BUILD YOUR
SALES
TRIBE

BUILD YOUR SALES TRIBE

SALES IN THE INFORMATION AGE

STEVE SCHRIER

unbound

First published in 2021

Unbound
Level 1, Devonshire House, One Mayfair Place, London W1J 8AJ
www.unbound.com
All rights reserved

© Sales Tribe Ltd, 2021

Text design by PDQ Digital Media Solutions Ltd

A CIP record for this book is available from the British Library

ISBN 978-1-78352-878-3 (paperback)
ISBN 978-1-78352-879-0 (ebook)

Printed and bound in Great Britain by Clays Ltd, Elcograf S.p.A.

1 3 5 7 9 8 6 4 2

For Wendy, Olivia and Arthur, and my father, Chris.

Contents

Introduction	1
1. Attitude and Approach	13
2. Basic Types of Sales Roles and How to Fill Them	43
3. Commission	71
4. Becoming an Expert	81
5. An Ideal Customer Profile	99
6. Pricing	105
7. The Sales Process	129
8. Engage	157
9. Finishing a Deal	195
10. Metrics, Targets and Measurement	209
11. Looking After Existing Customers	221
The Future	239
Index	243
A Personal Message from the Author	249
Acknowledgements	251
About the Author	253
Supporters	255

Introduction

What's in this book for me?

This book will tell you how sales has changed and how to succeed with selling in the Information Age now – and in the future. It will help your business deal with topics such as diversity and inclusion, ethics of selling, artificial intelligence (AI) and 'big data'. It will bring you practical advice from years of real-life experience to help you attract more business and look after your existing customers better through these disruptive times.

First, let me tell you a story...

There was this kid who loved computers. So he went to college and he studied electronics and computing. When he graduated, in the early 1990s, he went to work for a small tech company in the UK whose global headquarters were in the Bay Area of San Francisco. It wasn't a large company, it made controllers for the big videotape machines used to make television programmes – animation, special effects, post-production, that sort of thing. Sounds glamorous but the kid mainly did the crap

1

stuff that no one else wanted to do – technical support, fixing things, pulling cables, etc.

The kid quickly realised that if he learned how to sell the equipment and not just fix it, he would be able to travel regularly to various countries and see the world. So he convinced his boss to give him a shot and went into sales. He didn't even know that it existed as a job – no one had even mentioned it as a possible career path at school, and the people around him pretty much looked down on it as a profession.

Recognising the value of the kid, and of contributing to his sales education, his boss worked with him and went on to do the same for another Bay Area company that floated on Nasdaq (US Stock Exchange) in 1994. With their help this company went through fourteen record consecutive quarters of earnings after going public and became a billion-dollar company.

The kid was twenty-three and running all over the world learning how to sell and run a distribution channel. He was in a different country/city every week and having the time of his life. He worked with some amazing people and loved it. He also found – because he knew how the products worked, and why they were different from others – that he was good at it.

He moved on, out of sales, into more product-oriented roles. But it wasn't the same.

After several entrepreneurial failures and bad choices, in different industries, he ended up losing all the money he had left and needed to get a job to support his wife, baby son and two-year-old daughter. He knew he could sell so he went back to sales – this time selling direct to business customers on the management team of an Internet start-up, with a business model for a new age – and only a handful of customers.

It was very different – it wasn't as easy as before. He had to learn how the Information Age was transforming the world. Different customers with more diversity and new approaches. He looked around for books and advice but found none that fitted – one or two with something on the basics but a lot which were no longer relevant. So he had to work it out himself.

That was me. This is the book that I wished I had been able to read then. It is here for you so that you don't have to work it out yourself. In a world that is changing enormously I hope this book will be the guide for your business for now – and one that you will reach for in times to come.

How do you succeed?

The pace of change is increasing enormously, and commerce and business are being disrupted as never before. And it is not set to stop anytime soon.

A lot of entrepreneurs I have spoken to who have built successful businesses or management teams, and who belong to networks of high-growth, profitable companies say, 'Sales is a major problem ... We couldn't find anyone to do the sales function, so we had to do it ourselves.'

On closer examination, what they are really saying is that the whole sales function for their organisation isn't something that is working well for them, because they don't know how to set up and manage a suitable sales function for the world of 'big data' (commonly understood to mean the volumes of data captured in recent history regarding user behaviour) or artificial intelligence (AI).

Marketing connected to AI, technology and massive amounts of data is increasingly exploiting the Information Age to mean that most buyers are empowered as never before. Simple sales processes are disappearing. In this world 'sales' people are no longer required in many business-to-consumer (B2C) and simple business-to-business (B2B) situations; they are simply order takers, if they are human at all.

But in more complex sales, typically those that involve more than one interaction with the customer, sales are becoming more important than ever before for success. What is sometimes referred to as 'consultative selling' will have to be the basis of sales engagement along with an ethical approach.

Sales is at the forefront of diversity and inclusion strategies since it is imperative that any sales team is able to effectively connect with the people who work with their prospective customers.

As a result, an intelligent approach to sales is – and will increasingly become – a very significant differentiator for an organisation going forward.

Within this environment, there are thousands of inventive start-up companies whose aim is to take advantage of this period of uncertainty, create new business models and emerge as new leaders. In addition, there are large incumbent organisations that are grappling with modernising their position in the marketplace, in order to take advantage of these disruptive environments and maintain their dominant positions – or try and find new ones.

But what is the use of having a terrific product or innovative new service if you can't engage in a proper way with potential customers? As we rapidly move further into the Information Age, many people are unable to keep up with the pace of change, making it difficult to find good people to hire for any business, including salespeople.

More importantly, it is not the *function* of selling that needs addressing, but the whole process of how the sales function works in, and with, the other elements of an organisation, since an organisation structured to pick the right deals with the right customers will maximise opportunities away from the disruption, and will make innovators successful more quickly, with the right relationships to propel them to the forefront of their markets.

If you get the sales structure system right for *your* company, then, with some energy and investment, hiring people to work within it shouldn't be so difficult. This book will show you how.

It is imperative that the sales function for an individual business or organisation is structured to differentiate effectively, especially in a world where staff will rely heavily on technology to do a lot of the work for them.

Others, like you, can take a more intelligent approach and follow a process that works for them to deliver the best for their customers and themselves alike. They will go back to some of the basics and think differently in order to enable sales to be a modern, organised growth engine, dovetailed with other organisational functions to be the basis on which to succeed. Their salespeople need to be well equipped to deliver the best results – and that is where this book comes in.

How to use this book

This book and its supporting materials are designed to help business owners, start-up founders, entrepreneurs, shareholders and management teams put together an approach that drives the correct behaviour for their business – and allows them to find the right people to become part of their sales teams to make it work.

By following the practical steps laid out in this book, anyone can structure a strong sales function, and build, attract and maintain a first-class commercial approach, which operates in (relative) harmony with the other functions of the business to bring and maintain the right relationships and customers. That is, an approach which is able to make the right deals for a business and takes advantage of the age in which we are living – not suffer because of it.

After setting up the basics in this introduction, we deal with attitude and approach in Chapter 1. Here we start to uncover the mindset and the sorts of considerations that should be made in the approach to selling. This book is not designed to dictate a sales methodology, but it does seek to identify a correct mindset for commercial people and a structure for them to work within.

The next chapter deals with commercial roles and how to fill them. Here we discuss the types of characteristics of commercial people, diversity and inclusion, job descriptions and how to interview to fill those positions.

In Chapter 3, we explore commission, whether it should be paid, how it should be structured, the effect it can have and who should be eligible.

Next we discover why becoming an expert is a critical element in modern sales and how to establish your whole organisation as an authority in your business sector, to support your commercial efforts.

In Chapter 5, we explore the ideal customer profile and how to make that work for you – the crucial building block to working out which deals to sign for growth, success and internal harmony before you even engage with customers. This will ensure the deals on the table are deals you want to sign!

Next up we explore pricing. It is often a complicated element that people struggle to get right and can be influenced by a number of factors. It is important that money is not left 'on the table'.

A lot of people say, 'Make selling a process,' but what does that mean? The sales process is the subject of Chapter 7. It is important that you make the sales process suit you – not your customer relationship management (CRM) system. Here we also explore how to advance deals through the sales process.

Now we have worked out how we want to approach our commercial function, it is important to explore how to structure targeting and engagement with prospective customers to take them through the sales process established in the previous chapter. The Engage chapter (8) looks closely at that.

A lot of deals get stuck before they are finished – the Finishing a Deal chapter (9) explores how to get the deal over the line and some negotiation tactics for complex deals.

Sales are highly measurable and use metrics: metrics and targets will help you manage the team to execute the work you have done to create the process. This is discussed in Chapter 10.

Lastly, in the Looking After Existing Customers chapter (11), we look at account management. Often there is a 'Pareto principle' here where 80 per cent of revenues come from 20 per cent of existing customers, so it makes sense to try and maximise the relationships with all customers to attempt to change that and mitigate the risk associated with losing a big one. As deals get more complicated in the Information Age and people seek recurring revenue streams for products and services, looking after customers is paramount for success – even, in some cases, more than getting new business.

The final chapter offers a vision of why the future is bright for salespeople.

Below most sections in each chapter are projects and tasks to perform to adapt the advice to your business. Since every business is different, it is important that this works for you. The book is not the only resource; it is complemented by materials at the Sales Tribe blog (www.salestribe.blog/welcome) and exploration into deeper topics and discussions are referenced throughout.

I hope you get great value from this book and the other resources, and that it changes the way you do business forever. Happy selling!

Assumptions

In order to benefit from this book, an organisation needs to be in a basic position to act on information and make a plan.

The types of businesses that should benefit from this book

- This book is for the management of the organisation. It is designed to help business owners, entrepreneurs, shareholders and management teams, etc. put together an approach that drives the correct commercial behaviour for their business. It is also for the salespeople who need to execute the resultant plan.
- There isn't necessarily a difference between a small- or medium-sized company and a large one. The approach is the same, but just involves more or fewer people, politics and opinions. This book is aimed, however, at small-to-medium-sized (SME) organisations which are looking to set up or run a dedicated commercial function. This may also be a department of a large company that needs to adopt its own commercial approach.
- This book is mainly for organisations that need to make larger and more complex sales. Those are sales that require more than one sales call or interaction to make the sale

and, in all probability, some sort of ongoing relationship with the customer once the initial sale is over.

- The organisations have a decent product or service which has been 'productised'. It doesn't really matter whether this is a physical product that is manufactured (or someone else manufactures on behalf of the organisation), is something that is bought from someone else, value-added sold on, or is a service that is provided. It could also be something that is licensed to another person, such as software or intellectual property. Or any combination of these.

- The organisation already has one or more paying 'arm's length customer'; that is, a customer who is not a family member or a friend.

- There is some idea of the pricing or commercial model. This can just be a fixed price that someone has paid once in order to buy something. It can also be a revenue stream that is born through some sort of recurring payments. This is important as it means that the marketplace has accepted the product/service at a certain level.

- The current pricing of the product or service that is sold either needs to have a margin which makes the organisation a profit or there should be a clear way to make a profit from the sales as the business expands. Eventually, the organisation will need to make profitable sales; otherwise there is little point starting the activity.

- There is some sort of presentation/demonstration of what the organisation's product or service is or does.

- The organisation has the ability and willingness to sell/ deliver the product or service to more customers and grow the business. It needs to be the organisation, not just an individual manager, who has this ambition.

This book is about engaging with people properly and finding if there is a fit for both parties before entering a business relationship.

Definitions

- Suspect – an organisation that on the surface could be a potential customer but has not been matched to the seller's ideal customer profile (Chapter 5).
- Prospect – an organisation that has been through a set of qualification questions and fits an organisation's ideal customer profile (Chapter 5).
- Pipeline or funnel – a list of potential deals that shows how far through the sales process a customer is. The sales process is discussed in detail in Chapter 7.

1. Attitude and Approach

The first thing to be dealt with in any successful commercial organisation is what is going on inside the individual salesperson's mind when it comes to the commercial approach. These are the fundamental building blocks for success and cover a wide range of topics. It is very important that commercial people with this mindset are sought by management, or that this is instilled in them through clear company communication – usually a bit of both.

In this chapter we shall discuss:
- How to approach sales.
- How many deals are out there?
- Uncovering problems and developing empathy.
- Sell what you've got.
- Selling on price.

How to approach sales

First, it is important to examine how to approach 'sales' from the perspective of the individual. Often sales is perceived as a process whereby one loud, brash individual somehow forces their way into a situation with someone, where they present a product or service – in isolation, without any consultation upfront or based on conjecture – stating what they believe the features and benefits of the product or service to be to an individual or set of individuals.

Then they spend some time post-pitch aggressively convincing, persuading and defending their proposition until the prospect is either completely worn down to the point where they give in and buy, or they get fed up and stop or move on to a competitor. If the salesperson does this enough times, eventually they will be successful and find someone who will sign a deal with them.

Generally, this puts the prospect into a situation where they do not gain any value from the process of engaging with the salesperson. The typical image of salespeople is derived from this technique.

Even if slightly exaggerated, it is amazing how common this approach has been – or at least the perception of it. It only focuses on one person's objective, and that is the salesperson's. It is almost a coincidence if the product or service is a fit for the prospect. The customer is left to decide for themselves whether it works for them. This approach is not usually joined up with any other members of the salesperson's organisation or the strategic direction of a company trying to supply the products or service, except where the product or service is a manufactured commodity.

The outcome of this type of selling typically yields deals and relationships that start with distrust, become fractious and lack value as they go forward.

The digital age demands different behaviour. Salespeople need to provide much more value as part of the process, and link up with other members of the company selling the products or services, to make sure that what is sold is what will be delivered.

These individuals may well not be the same brash, loud individuals that society might expect to find as salespeople. In fact, it is becoming much more likely that the person who will be more successful in selling a product or service does not have those characteristics, but is a more considered and confident type of person; confidence coupled with real knowledge about what they are selling, the customers they are selling to, their competition and the market they are selling into. As such they have the ability to establish themselves and their organisations as credible experts who provide an honest appraisal of what is best for a customer and their company as a supplier.

In the Information Economy, salespeople need to approach the commercial-engagement process from a different perspective and work out whether the people (not normally one individual) and the organisation that they are talking to are in the right place to work with the product or service that the salesperson is representing. Customers will typically come from a wide spectrum of society, and management of the supplier will need to replicate that diversity and inclusion in their teams for the people they want to sell to. They will need to create true value on both sides, even going through the process before either party has decided whether or not to proceed.

The questions also form the basic toolkit from which to build a valuable sales process for the selling company and for the prospect, whether it results in a deal or not, and are the basis of a win-win situation.

PROJECTS & ACTIONS
DECIDE THE SALES APPROACH OF YOUR COMPANY

Questions contemporary companies and their sales organisations ask themselves:

- How do we want to be perceived as a sales organisation?
- Will we try and sell from the point of view of the customer?
- Will we try and establish meaningful relationships in which your company is considered an expert in its field?
- Will you attempt to build a deal-flow of quality partnerships which yield long-term results?
- How many deals do we need to close to make a difference, and what is the real target?
- What type of business should we be doing for the benefit of ourselves and our customers, so they become long-term relationships that yield a win-win for all parties?
- What do these deals look like? Who are they with?
- What should our 'pipeline/funnel' look like?
- How does the sales function work with the rest of our colleagues, and how will sales bring the deals that work for us as a unit, not just for the salesperson/team?
- What do good and bad customers look like to our organisation?
- If we decide to target and sign, for example, ten new customers in x time, what will our business look like then,

---

and how do we make sure those new customers fit with our existing business?
- What are the ethics around how we sell and how we treat our customers?

Answers to these questions should be established clearly in advance so as to empower the salesperson or people to deliver the right deals.

How many deals are out there?

One of the key principles of modern selling is the fact that the sales process (Chapter 7), and what happens outside and around it, needs to have value for both sides, even if no deal ultimately takes place. It is very easy for firms to make high targets and put pressure on salespeople, but how many deals are realistic?

Similarly, it is easy for salespeople to put themselves in the mindset whereby every deal is an opportunity which must be signed, regardless of whether it is right for the company that's selling or the people who are buying. This is the wrong way to begin any relationship. People can sense desperation and it puts pressure in the wrong area. This pressure changes the way that a salesperson engages with a potential prospect and ultimately can result in bad deals.

Rather, it is important that any salesperson and the organisation around them believe in a vast array of opportunities; a land where there are so many deals that one company or person would struggle to sign them all. So if one falls away, there will be another one just around the corner to add to the sales pipeline.

This changes the mental approach significantly. For the salesperson it means:

- Every deal that comes along doesn't have to be signed.
- The salespeople don't approach the process from an angle of desperation.
- The salespeople put themselves in a position where they can have a different dialogue with the potential customer, which explores how they and the customer can build success together.
- It is possible to say to a potential customer – and there will be situations when it should be said – that a deal *may not be right for the supplier organisation.*

There can be many reasons why this last situation might occur, but the most common is that the customer won't follow the sales process, or they want to chip away at the price when the supplier organisation has reached a place where it doesn't make sense to continue.

Whatever the reason, it is important that a prospective buyer understands that the supplier organisation is as much in the driving seat as they are when it comes to the two parties doing business. And this changes how the salespeople approach doing business with customers.

At this point it is also important to understand that there is a fine line between the feeling of abundance – that there are plenty of other fish in the sea – and *arrogance.* Arrogance is a sales killer.

It is important to make sure the salesperson's attitude comes across in the way they engage with a prospective buyer. They should manage their own expectations *first*, and remember that *they* can walk away – and should do if it doesn't work for the company, *but* for the right reasons.

Evidently, this is a place where salespeople and management might have a different opinion, especially where targets come into play. And, therefore, the supplier organisation should have a clearly defined process upfront that has buy-in from all involved. Then, when a decision is made, it is made for a clearly defined reason.

TIPS & NOTES

» There are always exceptions to any rule, but in general being able to say 'no' to customers for certain deals makes for a much better approach and, as a result, a company will sign better deals and establish better relationships which will yield more profits from its customers. If a prospective buyer expects a company to roll over and do everything they ask, it is important to change their attitude. After all, how will the supplier be able to control the process if the prospective buyer is allowed to run it? And if the supplier organisation isn't in control of the process, how can the deal be represented to colleagues as something that should be signed?

» If this attitude is adopted, then your salespeople will always be looking for a win-win situation and will quickly discover if there is no fit with a specific customer. Most importantly, it will stop the company signing deals with customers that are bad for it, without careful consideration.

Uncovering problems and developing empathy

Successful selling is and always will be mainly about one thing – that is, using a special tool; the most important special tool of selling. Ears!

But for a salesperson to use their ears, ask the right questions and *actually listen* to people takes a lot of effort. It is a skill that is built up over time and doesn't seem to be very common these days. Consideration should be given to this essential trait of a good salesperson:

- Listening can be mentally taxing and tiring, as anyone who has tried really listening when people talk can testify. Remembering someone's name when they say it. Remembering things people say about themselves, their business or the market – good salespeople store it away and remember it, or make a note of it somewhere if they find remembering it difficult.

- This may sound superficial, but it has real implications in the skill of selling, since listening to someone allows the salesperson to understand problems. Uncovering problems by asking questions and listening to the answers allows the salesperson to find a solution – and, most importantly, potentially uncover opportunities that seemingly did not exist before. This is the skill of sales.

- Like medical doctors, good salespeople become 'sales doctors' and that involves listening carefully to the patient – in this case, the prospective customer – and asking the right questions, as discussed in the sales process (Chapter 7).

- Management should make sure good salespeople establish an environment where the people or person trusts them enough to share intimate details about their situation. Good salespeople will ask questions to uncover the problems that a company has; this is the beginning of finding a solution and motivating them to change.

- Like a medical doctor, it can take a little while, and perhaps more than one meeting, to establish an environment in which someone will really talk. But the salesperson needs to establish a rapport in order to be able to ask the right questions. This involves treating someone with an element of respect without being submissive, desperate or gushingly complimentary.

- It is better for a salesperson to have a broad set of commercially relevant facts and to open a conversation by talking about those, then to develop an exchange of information over time. They should establish themselves as a questioner in the relationship, gradually working in more questions based on the answers that they receive so as to build up a picture.

But most of all, it is necessary for the salesperson to become an expert in what they are doing (Chapter 4), because most prospective customers will just want to get down to business and not talk about their favourite football team or their dog. This is where the set of questions asked is crucial.

And, in the Information Age, this is where generalists will struggle. Of course, not everyone wants to be open about often confidential information. And, just as they may not be completely honest with a medical doctor about the number of cigarettes they smoke, the alcohol they consume or the number of sexual partners they have had, a prospect may not be providing the salesperson with 100 per cent accurate information. This is where salespeople need to establish credibility over time to unlock the true picture.

Credibility comes from honesty and being seen as an expert in a particular business, so the prospective customer feels able to share relevant information.

TIPS & NOTES

» In some cases it is impossible to have a conversation that goes anywhere in the direction of meaningful dialogue – the prospective customer will simply refuse to engage any more than to ask about the supplier's product and then the price. A good salesperson is prepared for this and can explain something about why this information is required. Introducing the sales process (Chapter 7) that the supplier's organisation will need to follow to do a deal at this point may help. The start point is for the salesperson to explain that any deal begins with the supplier's organisation understanding more about the prospective customer's business and what fits for them.

» This process doesn't have to take long, but it might. It is important that the salesperson is not in too much of a hurry or they will come across as desperate or pushy. They will need to go at the pace of the suspect, like a good doctor with a patient. Some 'patients' may be confused and inarticulate, or simply not know, whereas others may be precise and straightforward, but not provide enough information. Good salespeople will be able to extract the information necessary to build a picture in which a deal can be explored, and recognise the fine line between being invasive with their questioning and obtaining relevant information. It is a skill that can be developed, although some people have a natural aptitude for it.

» If encounters are approached like this, salespeople will end up hearing not only about the professional problems of the individuals, but may also learn a lot about the company, colleagues and personal circumstances. It is important that this information is treated with the utmost care, since certain nuances in the information can change the situation a great deal. Notes must be made carefully and stored where they can be referred to for future meetings. They should be reviewed and verified at every opportunity.

» This information must also be regarded by a supplier's organisation as highly confidential. Betrayal of that trust or confidentiality can affect the credibility of the company – and that affects its ability to make deals.

Modern selling is more about relationships than ever before. Establishing a relationship where someone can share their professional problems and can be comfortable answering questions from salespeople involves careful listening, before the information can be used to tailor the conversation in order to find solutions. Once the problems have been identified, a supplier organisation is in a position to make a much more relevant pitch or presentation which generates a true motivation to change.

Empathy

The *Oxford English Dictionary* defines the word 'empathy' as 'the ability to understand and share the feelings of another'.

It is different from 'sympathy', which is defined as 'feelings of pity and sorrow for someone else's misfortune', but this is often confused with empathy.

Empathy dovetails with an ability to uncover opportunity. It is a strong trait for any salesperson. If someone can put themselves in the position of the buyer and also truly listen, it is a powerful combination in a sales context and can significantly affect the credibility of the conversation and the ability of a salesperson to ask the right questions.

Attention to detail

The *Star Wars* films comprise a story revolving around characters who can feel 'the Force'. The characters are very sensitive and can detect and act upon small changes in the Force, even though they may not truly understand its meaning or what it might lead to. Good salespeople have a similar characteristic – their 'Force' is the market they are selling into. They are immersed in it so that when they see the slightest change in detail or situation, they can pick up on it. Over time this gives them the ability to identify and put together nascent opportunities.

Obviously, there can be more telling details circulating around the customer, and having the ability to notice such things will also greatly affect sales competence; for example, the personal situation of the individuals, good or bad reports to the stock market, news stories, changes in the market that affect the customer directly, and so on.

All these things build a picture which can help find the customer's professional problems and put deals together.

PROJECTS & ACTIONS
LISTENING

- How do you and your sales function currently listen to your customers?
- How do you record information that is given to your organisation?
- Is this contained within a customer relationship management (CRM) system that also tracks your sales pipeline/funnel monitoring your sales process?
- Is it highly regarded and confidential, in a shared repository, or is it sitting in a person's head and/or inbox? This is a strategic asset of your business – make sure you treat it as such!
- A suggested assignment to try here is to task anyone involved in selling, and perhaps the whole organisation, with not listening to anyone for perhaps an entire day. When someone asks a question, don't listen to the answer, don't look them in the eye, etc. But be careful: it is very irritating, but it will show how important listening is.

How and when (and when not) to 'pitch'

What if a salesperson doesn't know his product/service well enough to present it? In today's business environment a salesperson who is unable to show a prospective customer a product/service first hand, or cannot speak with authority and in detail about it, is not really a salesperson at all. They should not only be unafraid to do all of the above, but should relish the opportunity, as well as know pretty much everything about it. It is a fundamental part of establishing credibility. It should be considered part of the job unless the subject matter is highly specialised or complicated, in which case another party can be brought in to help (but not to do the salesperson's job).

This is not a dirty job and it isn't something that should be avoided. Management's salespeople should have all the equipment and access necessary to do this in a self-contained way; if they haven't, they are wasting the prospective customer's, and everyone else's, time. A presentation, for example, should be ready to be made and should look polished. In addition, it should have been practised and rehearsed before the presentation proper. It should not rely on third parties such as Internet connections or firewalls, and it shouldn't need to have x, y or z to make it work.

Salespeople unwilling or not prepared to present their product or service in detail are all too common, and it is lazy and an obvious way of losing any kind of rapport with a prospective customer. How is that customer supposed to buy something if they can't see what they are buying, irrespective of how big the company is or how good its reputation?

Whatever the supplier is selling, the salesperson should be able to present the product or service in a way that a prospective customer can understand and relate to in a positive way. And it should be tailored to the needs of the customer uncovered by asking questions – not a pre-packaged, 'one-size-fits-all' approach.

There is also nothing worse than someone who will simply not stop pushing and demonstrating when it is completely inappropriate to do so. Making a product or service presentation should only be done with the mutual agreement that it is something the prospect wants to see, normally to cover the explicit needs developed out of questioning.

> **TIPS & NOTES**
>
> Good salespeople treat other people as human beings first. This means finding out about the status of the customer, as an individual, as well as the organisation, before launching into a pre-packaged presentation or product demonstration or pitch. Organisations that recognise this will arm their salespeople with the right tools to do their job.

TREAT PEOPLE AS HUMAN

We were trying to pitch to a big potential customer. I had identified the person I needed to speak to, in order to at least make a pitch. I had cold-called her many times, left her a lot of voicemails and managed to speak to her on a handful of occasions. She was friendly but very non-committal, and obviously took a lot of calls. She agreed to be on our email list, but I could see that she wasn't reading anything we sent her.

We attended a large annual conference and trade show frequented by most of the industry. Instead of having a stand inside the exhibition, we took a small suite in the hotel next door, which was a popular meeting place for the conference attendees, and invited prospects to meet us in this suite rather than the conference area as it was much quieter and you could have a proper conversation. (It was also much cheaper!)

Obviously, I had invited this person along and had even managed to set a date when she said she would arrive, at the end of the day. She was a little late but she did turn up with her boss, who was another one of the decision makers we would need on board. They started by being quite reserved and looked quite flustered as we ushered them into the suite and got them some coffee. We took it very easy and just spoke about them and their background, their experiences, etc. It was a nice relaxed conversation with a few jokes and a friendly tone.

Eventually, they started to open up and told us that the day had been a complete nightmare for them, as they had gone from one hard sales pitch to another. We were the only people who had treated them like human beings. Even though we were well over our allotted time with them, they stayed and talked through some of our offerings. Then they invited me to their offices after the show to meet the senior executive who looked after the business unit. Our approach meant we went on to have an amazing relationship with them and they became one of our best customers.

PROJECTS & ACTIONS
PRESENTATIONS AND PITCHES
- What does your pitch look like?
- Are you and your team empowered to make a meaningful presentation/demonstration, which really gives them something of value to the conversation?
- What is the appetite for showing off the product or service and answering a customer's questions about it?
- What set of questions will your salespeople ask before presenting your offering in context? Will these questions uncover opportunities over time and allow them to present

---

solutions, or are they just 'blunt instruments' that don't facilitate a conversation?
- If you have a slide show or presentation, how long is it? Does it really need to be that long? Does it facilitate asking the questions you need to be answered to establish whether someone is a good fit for doing business with your organisation? Is it clear and simple while presenting your expertise in the business area? Could it be replaced with a series of actual case studies?

Confidence and dealing with rejection

Confidence is a trait that is necessary in all good salespeople. Confidence changes a person's body language and their whole manner of approach.

- Having the confidence to approach strangers, to try to establish a relationship, is something that is difficult to ignore as a skill. There will be rejection and the timing is not always right, but confidence isn't necessarily something that comes from being brash and loud. It can be built up and learned, and even the most introverted individual can become a confident authority and competent salesperson.
- First and foremost, there needs to be a belief that the product or service that the person is selling is of high quality and benefit to another party; that there is an abundance of potential customers out there that will gain incrementally by becoming a client of the salesperson's organisation.
- The knowledge of the salesperson and their place in the supplier organisation is also of major importance. If the salesperson has little knowledge of the industry they are

selling into, and is unaware of other products and services on the market, the competition and how the company fits into this industry, this can affect their confidence levels significantly – or lead to the type of shallow confidence that becomes detrimental to a sales approach.

- Management should ensure the salesperson holds a reasonable level of intelligence and domain knowledge, to empower them to establish authority through credibility and make sure they are well equipped to engage with the prospect. Misguided education in a market can be worse than none at all – if a salesperson espouses great knowledge with authority and confidence which is plainly wrong to the others in his company, it will remove almost all opportunity for him to develop opportunities further.

- Having said that, the greatest confidence of all is the confidence to make mistakes. Mistakes in approaching people and businesses, or making assumptions about the state of a business and so on. This is where a salesperson must be able to make assumptions but then correct them, in order to build up a true picture of what is happening and the opportunities with a target company and the challenges they face.

- Teamwork is imperative here; management should ensure a salesperson is supported and work with the salesperson or people to make the most of the sales activities. The business should always learn as the landscape changes, especially in modern times. The sales functions of a business normally see market changes first and these should be captured and shared. Salespeople are bound to make mistakes since they are not in control of all the moving parts, and it is important an organisation understands that and has the ability to learn from it as a business.

- Some people have a natural energy and confidence level that comes with their personality. They often make good salespeople but only if they also have the ability to take on the ethics and approach of a company, and to learn about the product and market in which they are working in depth, so that the opening of a conversation can lead to an opportunity to take it further. This establishes credibility alongside confidence. There is more on confidence here: www.salestribe.blog/confidence

---

PROJECTS & ACTIONS

Developing confidence. Here is something to try with your whole organisation, not just the salespeople. 'Comfort challenges' are challenges which generally take people out of their comfort zone for a period to help them get over their fears. This helps them to deal with the fear of rejection you have to overcome to be a good salesperson. Comfort challenges can sometimes be daunting so it is a good idea to do them together as a team and make it fun.

There are many of these that can be explored on the Internet, but here are my five favourites:

1. Lie down in a crowded place for thirty seconds at a time. If someone asks you if you are OK, then you can say 'yes', but make sure you stay where you are for the full thirty seconds.

2. Choose a day when you will be in a busy area, then whenever you buy anything, including food or coffee, try to negotiate with the person selling it to get a discount. Any discount is good, but try for 20 per cent. This is especially good if there is a long queue behind you.

---

continued

3. Sign up to perform a public-speaking engagement on something non-work related; something you have never spoken about publicly before. The speech should be for at least five minutes to a decent size audience (fifty+).
4. Say 'yes' to *everything* for a week. (This one also teaches you how important it can be to say 'no' sometimes!) Extra rules can be added here for personal safety!
5. Look people in the eye when you are talking to them.

Intelligent persistence is gold

In addition to confidence, it is imperative that there is a level of persistence in the salesperson. Confidence and persistence are not the same thing. Most people are not in buying mode all the time, unless their job is in 'procurement' or some sort of buying role. So timing is an important part of sales.

Many people in a prospect's organisation may work in a team and choosing, managing and dealing with suppliers is only one part of that role. In the Information Age there are generally more people to deal with to finish a deal.

A large part of a sales job is about working the relationship with the people that a supplier perceives fits an ideal customer definition (Chapter 5), to show them the supplier organisation is the right business for a buyer to work with. To ask the questions that uncover an opportunity for both parties. This can take some time (and some money) to achieve, depending on the customer. Persistence is a great skill for any salesperson to have, in an intelligent context – but obviously there is a line between persistence and being downright annoying.

There are a lot of views on persistence, but a general rule would be that an individual in a prospective customer organisation should be contacted at least five or six times before moving on. Things aren't always what they seem. It is important to keep chipping away, building those relationships. And a good salesperson never writes off anyone unless they are sure that they will never be part of a process.

GOLDEN PERSISTENCE

I was a salesperson for a company in telecoms, which sold technology that the phone manufacturers embedded in their handsets to enhance the phones' functionality. It was pretty cool stuff and I knew if I got to the right people, there was at least a conversation to be had. Therefore, my targets were large manufacturers of these devices.

At the time Nokia was the largest mobile-phone manufacturer in the world and was firmly established in my Europe, Africa and Middle East territory, with headquarters in Finland and offices all over Europe.

So I set about getting to know the Nokia people. I took every opportunity to meet them and joined them at conferences, and so on, and became quite well networked into their organisation. What I found was they all had vague or spurious job titles which made it impossible to determine anyone's real job role. They were also permanently restructuring, which meant people appeared to move job every month or so, and the most senior people weren't decision makers in any meaningful way – at least that is how it seemed.

I met a bunch of great guys from their company, travelled a lot and yet it seemed that I hadn't made any progress. Then I landed a small deal with them. It was with a new product line they had; an experiment – not quite the massive deal we had wanted but we did it anyway. It took a long time to get through their legal process and negotiate a contract, but eventually we signed it. Their experiment didn't really work and we didn't make much from it. It was quite frustrating, but that's the way it goes sometimes. At least we had some sort of relationship with them. We repeated this process a couple of times, but still the numbers weren't great for what we were providing to the largest potential customer in the business.

Then, two years in, I was suddenly called to a meeting at their Copenhagen office. I had been there before, but was confused as I thought any sizeable action happened in Finland. When I arrived, I met primarily with the guys I had met two years previously, who explained to me that they actually ran one of the largest divisions of Nokia on the consumer side, and always had. They also explained that they never simply jumped into bed with suppliers they didn't know very well, but expected to develop a relationship, so two years was roughly the minimum time they took to establish a relationship before they would think about doing a bigger deal.

From that moment on, I had a completely different relationship with the right people in the organisation.

PROJECTS & ACTIONS

- How many contacts do you/your sales team make before you give up?
- If you give up now, when do you revisit? It may just not be the right time.

Storytelling

For thousands of years information and knowledge have been relayed between people using stories. Long before computers, mobile phones and technology, people used stories as a way of making effective and memorable communication. Jokes and anecdotes are stories. Most religious texts are a selection of stories and most teachers use stories as a good way to engage with their pupils. Quite simply, people are used to good stories as an authoritative way of receiving and sharing information.

Good salespeople are good storytellers. The ability to put across things that are personal to them, including in a business context, will always be more memorable than dry detail. Presentations which include good stories will go down much better, and be significantly more memorable. If they can be informative and funny, so much the better. Questions that begin with a story to frame them for context will often receive a much more relevant response.

Some people are born with a natural ability to tell a story, but to an extent this is also something that can be learned. A lot of it has to do with attention to the detail of the story; getting it right and containing the relevant amount of facts.

Introducing statistics through storytelling can help

establish credibility, providing they are believable and have been worked through. But the most important aspect is timing, and how and when people are introduced and then built up as the reason for the story.

TIPS & NOTES

This is a vast topic and one we could discuss for the remainder of this book (see www.salestribe.blog/storytelling which points to resources and guidance on storytelling).

PROJECTS & ACTIONS

Consider how you establish credibility and what stories you and your team tell to aid you in establishing the people in your company as experts and helping others understand individuals, products, services and your company.

Effort and energy

There are no shortcuts to selling! There is no hack. The top salespeople work very hard. Although it might seem like it will be easier in the future, it will only become increasingly harder in the new economy to try and close deals. It is hard work trying to establish new relationships, build credibility within them, deal with rejection and generally persist. Listening all day is tiring as well as rewarding.

Most people, especially those in the buying seat for a company, don't have unlimited energy. What they have they will use professionally to do their job and make themselves look good. In general, they will follow the path of least resistance, unless there is something in it for them.

Often it is a big hassle for anyone to consider changing

providers in the first place, so why do it now and with a company/product/service? It is up to the salesperson and their whole organisation to make it simple and that requires energy: energy to be around before any process starts; energy to establish whether a sales process can begin; energy to ask the right questions in the sales process and uncover problems which motivate the customer to change; and, most importantly, energy to actually finish the deal when the process is at its end. Management and salespeople should focus a lot of energy on that last 10 per cent of the process, or the actual process is meaningless.

People who have natural energy about them and a 'get-up-and-go' approach will generally be much better at sales than others – this is a fact of life. But, ultimately, this is only the case if they are also focused on finishing a deal. A person can have an amazing network, spend a lot of time at events with people in the industry and be everyone's friend, but if they are not buyers, or not likely to be buyers in the future, then it isn't really sales!

However, it doesn't mean that good discipline can't be developed around an organisation's work culture to make sure sales focus is on these tasks. Management should look to exploit (in a nice way) the outgoing nature of a personality and combine it with a well-worked pattern that brings the deals to a close.

Management should be able to quickly discover whether someone is going to be able to bring the business the organisation wants; or just be a walking/talking expense account with a lot of contacts.

BOLDLY GO WHERE OTHERS DON'T

One of our biggest customers was located in a country to which we had to fly out once every quarter to meet them. We had an excellent relationship and it was always a good meeting followed by a nice dinner or social activity that perpetuated the relationship. Most other suppliers also visited this customer in the same way. However, I noticed that there was a much smaller customer located a couple of hours' train ride outside the city we visited. As I was there anyway, I made contact with them and tagged on a visit to them each time as part of my trip. It didn't take long and just required the effort involved to go and see them, which I could do by a relatively minor detour. But no other supplier bothered to do this. We started doing some business and rapidly became a major supplier for them, and they gave us premium placement within their products solely because of the way we treated them. More importantly, the people I was primarily visiting went on to become senior executives at a much bigger customer and that allowed me to have a great rapport with them in that role, which developed into a much bigger revenue stream.

PROJECTS & ACTIONS

- How does it feel to sell in your company?
- Is it a fun activity which people embrace and where there is healthy competition between the salespeople or other areas of the company?

- Do people feel empowered with an attitude to chase down a deal?
- Are they actually chasing down a deal or just hanging out with people who are never going to buy anything from your company?
- Is doing business with your company and sales team like wading through thick mud? If it is, how do you change that? How can your team be energised to go out and get the sales you want?

Sell what you've got

There will always be new versions of a product or plans for the delivery of enhancements to a service. It is very easy for salespeople to be distracted into delaying and talking about the new versions of something that is coming. If this is allowed to happen, then finishing deals and actually starting a relationship is always going to be difficult, especially in the Information Age. It means that a supplier potentially develops a deal-flow that is reliant on the company always delivering the next version of something, and so business today is difficult.

In a world that is changing at pace, it is easy to slip into a situation where the next version of anything will be presented and, naturally, that is what the customer will want. It is therefore very important that, even if the rest of the company is focused on a new and enhanced product or service, management should ensure the sales effort is focused always on what can actually be sold and delivered right now.

Of course, there are many examples of products that have been shipped before they are fully ready, as well as deals that have been done for products and services that don't actually exist at that time. This has varying success for the companies involved and in larger deals, where there are a lot of ancillary pieces, such as a large technology platform deal with many integrations of third-party systems, it is probably not possible to do the deal without there being lots of things that can't be delivered on day one.

Having a clear understanding of what will be delivered is imperative and selling what is available today wherever possible will yield the most success.

It is obviously sometimes good to discuss roadmaps or timelines when other functions, features, services or enhancement may come along, especially with important existing customers or strategic partners. However, keeping salespeople focused on selling what they have will provide the best return and the least confusion.

Selling on price

One approach to selling is just to be the company that is selling the cheapest product or service in the market. The sales message can be simply that the company's products or services are cheaper than everyone else's.

But is that really true? Is it possible for the company to produce the same thing more cheaply, sell it to the same target audience and still make good money?

And what happens when the competition then reduces their price to meet this new competitive price point? This is often called a 'race to the bottom' and happens in many markets.

However, pricing should be seen as the last line of defence – insofar as the organisation is able to avoid a head-on discussion purely about price. Introduce other elements to the customer before it reaches this stage: service, delivery, value and so on. Pricing should be reduced only when there is good reason and it has been forced upon the situation.

As much as the company is able, the target pricing for products and services should be neither the most expensive nor the cheapest, but somewhere in the mid–top range. If the supplier company is striving to deliver a good product and/or service, this should be where money can be made. Pricing is discussed in more detail in Chapter 6.

TIPS & NOTES

» It is easy to reduce a price to get a deal, but it is nearly impossible to increase it.

» Save reductions to the last minute. Don't allow constant chipping away at the pricing.

» Avoid 'negotiating against yourself'. When a customer repeatedly just says 'no' to pricing and tells you to come back with a better offer, instead ask them to counter-offer so you can see how far away you are.

» Your sales team needing to discount to close deals can be a sign of one of two things:
  • they are competitive and this discounting is finding the true market price for the deal;
  • they are lacking in a more proactive sales ability to discover true customer needs and present value – and this is costing you money.

2. Basic Types of Sales Roles and How to Fill Them

Defining roles well and finding the right people are powerful methods to achieve sales goals for an organisation.

In this chapter we will discuss:
- Hiring to create skills, not find talent.
- Types of salespeople needed for a business.
- Questions and tasks for management to use in interview.

Increasing the revenues of a supplier company can only be achieved by:
1. Getting new customers (new business).
2. Making new and existing customers buy more.
3. Customers buying more products and services more often.
4. Raising prices.

All these functions fit firmly in the 'sales' area.

Hiring to create skills, not find talent

There is a difference between talent and skills. Skills are something that can be gained, usually through work, often hard work, and some persistence. Talent is something that comes naturally to someone. It isn't unusual to hear that 'talent is in short supply'.

Looking to employ the most talented people creates a self-fulfilling prophecy – there will never be enough of them to go around. It creates a 'talent shortage'. Obviously, if the aim is to beat the world record in an egg-and-spoon race, it would make sense to look for someone who has a natural talent for running with balance. Or at least one of those characteristics with the expectation they would be able learn the other – most likely a good runner first. Then with some coaching this person may reach the top of their game at egg-and-spooning, provided they have the inclination to put the effort in.

With sales, some people are naturally better than others at elements of it, as discussed in Chapter 1, Attitude and Approach, as well as in this chapter, but hiring someone with perfect grades who has never failed at anything for a sales position is unlikely to yield success. That is, unless they are prepared to learn the same sales skills as another person.

Problem solving and listening are the very top characteristics for sales in the Information Age. There is no talent shortage – businesses need to find the people who are willing to learn how to do it, to put the effort in – and support them with a system that makes sense for their organisation. This may take some time and effort.

The other major management consideration should be diversity – do their salespeople 'match' their customer base? It is important that they do to maximise the opportunity to make sales from the outset.

How do organisations find these people? Look at what they have done before. Have they learned something difficult before? Have they failed but tried again and succeeded over time? Do they have some proper examples of this? Do they listen to what management says, or writes, and adapt their responses accordingly? Do they understand what taking a sales role means? Do they demonstrate enthusiasm and a general aptitude to be able to perform those functions?

With some basic criteria it should be possible for businesses to find the right people to sell for them. To represent the company in the marketplace – its culture, integrity and approach to business. They may well already be working with the company.

This does not necessarily mean those who have been selling somewhere else will fit another organisation either, but they may do. Hiring people who are willing to learn and persist is what is critical to success in sales roles now.

Types of salespeople needed for a business

It doesn't really matter how these functions are labelled in a business. For some reason no one wants to be called a 'salesperson' any more. Absurdly, 'sales' seems to be a 'dirty' word and a number of synonyms are often chosen instead. That's fine, but there are fundamental sales functions that need to be allocated and measured. It may be that there are dedicated teams for each one, or one person doing it all, or somewhere in between – it doesn't matter much. But the following are the fundamental roles that deliver success. Thinking about them as separate functions, measuring them and having a plan for each of them, is important. Often these skills are for different types of people.

Sales, new business, 'hunting'

One assumption of this book is that someone reading it wants to grow their customer base, sell more products/services and/ or establish new revenue streams. This is the sales or 'new business' function.

People who are great in this area can have different characteristics from other parts of the sales activity – they can be very different from anyone else in an organisation.

What comes to mind when someone says 'salesperson'? This function is responsible for targeting suspects, converting them to prospects and, ultimately, taking those that seem good for both sides through a sales process to conclude a deal, which is then delivered by the wider organisation.

Key sets of metrics and targets should be developed to monitor and report on sales and their likely contribution to the company in terms of revenues for projects delivered, as discussed in Chapter 10.

If the sales responsibility is included as part of other jobs, or not designated as a separate role, then that's OK, but the same principles should apply as if they are, and, with the new business role, having specific individuals with a focus on selling without distraction is always desirable.

There are two types of valuable people here:

1. The Hunter/'Closer'

> **TIPS & NOTES**
>
> Generally, a supplier company should not have people doing this job who are not focused on it 100 per cent.

Typically, these people will:

- Be confident, and won't be afraid of rejection, upsetting people or simply walking up to and talking to them.
- Not have a problem phoning or approaching someone they don't know.
- Have a positive mentality and be intelligently persistent in their approach (without being a pain).
- Have lots of friends and enjoy socialising.
- Be intelligent individuals, able to handle themselves in many different social situations.
- Be able to establish themselves as credible individuals, as people to do business with.
- Be quite disruptive with other staff – distracting them and getting them to do things they shouldn't be doing.
- Not document everything as well, or in as timely a fashion,

as may be desired, and may not follow procedures correctly.

- Will have a strong interest in making money, identified by the interview process (see below).

- Have a target, which should be achievable, and be rewarded by management if they exceed that target. As a very basic rule of thumb – and actually measuring people like this openly is problematic because it creates false ceilings – the target should be at least three to four times their total compensation package, including all costs.

- Have clear sets of metrics by which they know they will be measured, and rewarded, and it is also imperative that monitoring actually takes place and there are clear consequences if these metrics aren't hit (see Chapter 3, Commission).

- Be provided by management with a clear path, with no confusion, regarding how they should bring deals to the organisation, so that the organisation is able to work on existing projects, business, etc. and only take on the workload of new customers when it is appropriate. (We will examine this in more detail in Chapter 7, The Sales Process.)

- Not be office-bound 100 per cent of the time, but should have clear times when they can be in the office to perform certain functions such as making calls, appointment setting and researching.

- Make noise by being on the phone, etc. and to need to be able to have confidential conversations, presentations, etc. with customers, which may mean they need access to a private room.

- Have a clearly designated regular time where they

can learn from people internally about new product/
service innovation, and clearly identified people to talk
to regarding the wants and needs of potential customers
as they go through a sales process. If this does not exist,
management should expect they will be disruptive to their
colleagues while trying to do their job or they won't be able
to bring many deals.

- Management should ensure the education process, and
their ability to understand it, is significant: if salespeople
spend their time getting to a suspect/prospect and then
can't talk to them properly about an opportunity, it is
usually a wasted activity.

TIPS & NOTES

» Good salespeople need good management. Perhaps more
than any other area in an organisation, if salespeople are
not focused they will typically spend a lot of time working on
things other than sales. Sales are difficult and breaking down
barriers and getting in front of the relevant people is hard. It
is only natural that they might be easily distracted by other
tasks. It is up to the management of the company to make
sure that doesn't happen by having clear policies in place.

» If someone is found who is able to 'smash down doors'
and sign amazing deals, but who won't complete the
paperwork, won't adhere to reporting on the metrics
(even though they might be hitting them) and won't report
in when they are supposed to, then this may be a good
problem!

» If that person is so disruptive that they negatively impact
everyone else, it is usually not a good thing. Having one
stellar salesperson and no one else, or mediocre ones, is
not good for long-term success.

---

continued

» Barriers should be clearly communicated, and support mechanisms put in place to make sure the information needed from the salesperson back to the business exists, and that a process is being followed.

» People who can open a conversation but are *unable* to talk credibly with a customer about a product or service can often be damaging to an organisation. It is therefore important to find a balance.

» Often, in teams of salespeople, a sales coordinator or administrator is put in place to be the conduit through which information flows, although this person can have a much wider responsibility than that. This allows management of an organisation to deal with different characters, apply processes and monitoring and get the most out of the approach in this book.

A great 'hunter' is:
- Highly competitive.
- Intelligent.
- Persistent.
- Keen to finish deals – but may need help to close them.
- Keen to earn lots of money – and spend it.
- Social/empathetic – can listen.
- Knowledgeable about their product/service and market.
- Able (albeit often reluctantly) to handle rejection and accept failure.
- Passionate, aggressive, motivated and energetic.
- Emotionally detached.
- Involved in, or has played, team sports.
- Possessed of an ego that needs feeding.

2. Pre-Sales/'Opener'

There is a potential role, depending on the structure of the team, which is sometimes referred to as 'pre-sales' or 'inside sales'. This person is responsible for following up on leads, or in some cases creating them, and doing some of the initial qualification discussed in Chapter 7, The Sales Process.

- Some of the best people who are good at going out and starting a conversation – 'openers' – are pretty difficult to manage. It is important to understand the character of these people.
- Not all people are good at moving the deal along from the initial introduction to a proper conversation and sometimes prefer, or need, to take on a role where they hand over a relationship once it gets to a specific stage in the sales process.
- Typically, a pre-salesperson is in the office most of the time but communicates with potential customers remotely – by phone, email, social media, etc. to create/process leads.
- It is very important that this person is well educated about all new potential methods of contacting suspects as many more become available and others die.
- Pre-salespeople and hunters can work well together if one feeds the other and they agree on those roles. If they are competitive with one another in an unhealthy way, think they can do the other person's job better, or one isn't doing their job well, then it can be a recipe for disaster.
- There can be some complicated elements here, such as who receives the commission if the pre-salesperson identifies a deal which is later closed by the hunter. Policies should be worked out upfront that are clearly understood.
- Some large organisations, such as Google, use their

pre-sales teams to close 'small' deals while passing on the large, enterprise-style deals to specific colleagues.
• A pre-sales role can often be used to incubate a great 'hunter'.

Business development

These days people who do the selling are often called, or call themselves, 'business developers'. Actually, consideration should be made for a much more strategic role for those considered as 'business developers'. Something that is an important commercial role in a company, but isn't the same as new business 'sales'. Business development should be about strategic partnerships and this may be the primary type of salesperson required for some types of businesses. Sometimes this is called 'corporate development'. It doesn't much matter what it is called but it should be recognised as a slightly different skill set and approach for some companies.

STRATEGIC DEVELOPMENT

Apple doesn't make the iPhone. The iPhone is made by Apple pulling together technologies and expertise from other companies. Indeed, it is said that Apple has over 200 suppliers able to put their products together. Some of these will be highly strategic partnerships, where very sensitive and highly confidential information is shared, but they add value by putting the products and services together in a way that produces mass-

appeal products; i.e. the relationship is 'accretive' – greater than the sum of its parts. Someone needs to be responsible for these types of arrangements and it could be said that this sits firmly as a 'business-development' function.

Lego completely reinvented itself by making deals with film studios and brand owners, and aligning itself with all things popular with kids (and a lot of adults). It is now the largest toy company in the world when in the early 2000s it was almost bankrupt. They have used these deals to launch their own brands alongside them and are now reducing their reliance on these brands. This is another function that could be put in the 'business-development' category.

CEOs of new public businesses are often pushed to use the cash they have raised on the stock market to acquire other businesses. This is because the organic growth of companies is often not fast enough for shareholders. So a way of achieving growth in addition to core products is to acquire the profits of complementary businesses that may also add tangible value to other parts of an existing business. This means mergers and acquisitions (M&A). Often this is strategic and the most senior people in the organisation will be involved in these transactions, but the deals themselves are commercial in nature and good 'business-development' people should be responsible for doing these deals.

Often the organisation's products and services are

able to be packaged with another person's product or service to bring additional revenue streams without it being a 'secret' component, as in the Apple example above, but more of an alliance that provides more value for a customer if things are brought together. It can take a lot of networking and a different type of persistence for the business-development person since there often won't be an obvious deal for either party initially, although exploratory conversations can take place which will yield opportunities for both sides.

Someone must make the deals and manage them, and this leads to these strategic relationships – uncovered, executed and managed by 'business development' people. It is a much more strategic approach to commercial engagement, and takes a slightly different kind of skill. These people are also sociable, like salespeople, and there is a lot of crossover, but they have large networks and are well connected at all levels in different industries, so they can bring to an organisation deals that are not just normal sales deals. Business development deals often take a lot longer to set up and have a different process from sales. Great business-development people are a breed apart from normal salespeople and can be very valuable to an organisation at a senior level.

Allowing salespeople to try and do both business development and sales can distract them from the sales task at hand. Keeping them separate where possible, depending on the characters involved, can make for a good strategy if resources allow.

Some characteristics of a great business developer:
- Has a wide, large and expanding network.
- Is analytical.
- Is intelligent.
- Plays the longer game but is still persistent.
- Is strategic.
- Knows several markets well, but not necessarily the detail.
- Is not used to accepting rejection or failure.
- Has a legal or accountancy background.
- Doesn't like rejection or going in cold.
- Doesn't need a team.
- Wants to work at the most senior level.
- Wants to win big, strategic deals.

Sales account management, 'farming', commercial customer service

An organisation that already has customers, and wants to grow the relationships with these customers in terms of products and/or services they may take from it, requires sales-focused account managers. 'Sales-focused' because sometimes account managers are used to provide a form of customer service which doesn't necessarily involve trying to expand the relationship commercially. That is, not a sales-focused account management function.

- Account management can be a key area of connection between a supplier company and a customer – there should always be some sales element to it or it could overlook or waste many opportunities to grow revenues.

- It doesn't have to be a 'hard sell'. Mostly, it is better if it isn't. Instead, looking for ways of increasing revenues with these relationships often provides more growth than new business. Some companies see that 80 per cent of the revenues of the company come from 20 per cent of their existing customers, which can pose a significant risk. Expanding other existing relationships helps mitigate that risk.

- There is often some debate about whether there really is a difference between 'hunters' – the new business salespeople – and 'farmers', the account managers. This is down to the individual organisation but, in general, the most success can be obtained by treating them as different skill sets where people who are good at one thing may not be so good at the other. It doesn't mean one person can't do both jobs for a time but, ideally, they should be separated.

- Increasingly in the Information Age the successful coordination of multiple offerings of a supplier to deliver a solution is the way to grow the customer relationship. This is where a good account management function comes in. If selling a product or service means coordinating multiple parts of a business internally and then transitioning to a long-term relationship where there is an ongoing involvement, then good account managers are essential as a final part of the sales process, to take the relationship forward. (See Chapter 7.)

- The account management function should provide a day-to-day sales relationship between a supplier and customer organisation.

- The best account managers are those who see themselves as the customer's champion within their own organisation.

They are constantly looking at the customer's business, trying to find ways to improve their engagement and how their products will make a difference to the customer's life.

- Great account managers know all the key stakeholders in a customer's organisation and are able to facilitate seamless and easy connections between the customer and the functions within their business. They are also able to offer strategic and tactical assistance to the customer.

- Account management teams should be prepared to 'do the job' of the person who is receiving the product or service in the customer organisation, i.e. think as if they were the customer themselves. This has to be executed carefully if it is to work, but over time customer's staff will gravitate naturally towards the easiest option – the path of least resistance. If account managers make the people they work with look amazing to their peers and management, it can only increase their reliance on the account managers' products or services and the supplier.

TIPS & NOTES

Some organisations are structured so that they recognise new purchases from existing customers as new business. This means that the new business salespeople are responsible for all new revenue streams, even if the organisation has supplied the customer before. That works well if the products and services sold are one-offs and don't require a long-term relationship to be nurtured through different people in a supplier.

Characteristics of a great account manager:
» Is able to handle complex and difficult situations and solve problems.

---

continued

» Can absorb and understand detailed materials relative to a business and present them back in a clear and digestible fashion.

» Knows a product or service in depth or has demonstrated the ability to learn it elsewhere. Can prove that in an interview situation.

» Displays and demonstrates empathy.

» Is analytical; can take numbers and other data and present conclusions from them.

» Focuses on, and is proud of, the quality of relationships, both internally and externally.

» Understands the strategic importance of their role in the bigger picture.

» Has a network of close friends and business acquaintances but is not normally the leader. Is happy to follow.

» Not used to accepting rejection or failure. Can handle tense situations with support, but generally doesn't like confrontation.

» Is not happy alone; wants to work as part of a team.

» Is happy to be given tasks and able to execute them.

» Can suit those with a project-management or consulting background.

HOLDING OUT FOR THE RIGHT PERSON

When building a company with which I was involved, every colleague was critical to the company (as they are for most small-to-medium-sized businesses), and we couldn't afford to carry one substandard employee. When recruiting for one role – an account manager (the type of salesperson who looks after existing customers) who would deal with half of our best customers — I set a test which was basically doing the day-to-day job: examining some numbers; presenting some findings and recommendations; demonstrating a new product; and generally making representations as if we (my colleagues and I) were a customer in an interview situation. Sounds obvious and simple, right?

The brief was detailed and contained all the relevant information to give us what we needed, and before we saw the person they had passed some basic vetting criteria. Our business was in a new sector and we had a new business model which needed to be understood and supported through the techniques we had developed to keep our success coming.

We went through lots of people: some of the candidates were even doing this kind of job for our competitors; others had the most expensive educational backgrounds money could buy. We couldn't find anyone who could even get close!

My colleagues complained to me that we would never find anyone able to pass the test, that it was too hard, we were overloaded with work so we should just hire the next best person who came along. But I was adamant. If we didn't have the right person, then all of us would end up carrying the workload or, more likely — and worse — micro-managing that person to make sure the job was done to our standards.

It was six months before the right candidate walked into the room.

TIPS & NOTES
INTERVIEW QUESTIONS TO ASK AND TASKS TO SET

The aim here is not to replace the cultural, ethical and other processes an organisation employs to bring people on board. Similarly, there is an assumption that there is an induction process which takes new members of staff through the sales processes that are in place, the metrics and monitoring, and how they are expected to behave. Hopefully, these have also been developed through the topics presented in this book.

In order to assist in the process, some suggested questions to ask are listed below. But first some notes and tips.

» When hiring salespeople, consideration should be given to the fact that they are going to be the face and voice of an organisation – a lot of the time this will be when management is not around. So, in general, it is not a good idea to be in a hurry, even if there are burning business issues to hire people who will take a sales role. The hiring process should be structured so that it acquires the best person for an organisation.

» Typically, this is not a fly-by-night, 'quick-buck-following', smart-talking person, but someone who gels with an organisation in the role and with its people enough to provide and develop their expertise.

» The person should be actively tested on what they claim and care should be taken to ensure that there is a probation period of at least three months, which can be extended if necessary.

» Since it is difficult to find good salespeople, consideration should be given to widening a search to include people who know the products or service an organisation is providing but wouldn't naturally call themselves a 'sales' person. After all, once an organisation has developed its methodologies and structure, as described in this book, it will have a very clear picture of the person it wants and how it wants them to act, which should make it easier to identify the type of person who will fit. They may not be doing a sales role at the time. Some of the best salespeople have come from other roles.

» For the first phase, a list of questions should be set that will enable an organisation to filter the first candidates. At this stage, using some Internet-based video interviewing software for each of the candidates may be considered. This works by the candidate asking a series of questions, using the camera of their computer or phone/tablet, which are then recorded by the Internet service. Time can be limited and this allows a recruiter to review at their leisure without having to have a phone call or meeting. This can save a lot of time and there are many services available now (see www.salestribe.blog/video-interview-software for a post on using this powerful method of interviewing in your hiring process for salespeople).

» Management can provide materials about a product or service that can be learned by the candidate, and then ask them to a meeting in order to present the team face to face. By this stage, this is normally a small number of candidates.

» Standard interview questions are generally terrible because people are prepared for them. Try and move them outside their comfort zone. Create a safe haven for sharing information so that it is possible to learn about their lives, their current job and their ambitions.

» Their passion and what it is like for them working right now should be explored. If they have no passion for anything close to what is required in the role, it is unlikely that a passion will emerge while working in this job.

» Information provided should be meticulously recorded and checked for accuracy. If a claim is made about something they have done, further examples and details proving that they actually did it themselves should be sought, particularly if they claim success with specific numbers or deals. Make them responsible for providing evidence of something they claim.

continued

» References should be obtained from at least five people who may be consulted:
  - one personal reference, who can be asked about their character;
  - one former colleague, who can be asked about their work and relationships with other colleagues;
  - three customers they have worked with.

» Profound reference-checking is essential and not just of what is provided – references other than these should also be sought. There are many resources for this, but one way is to ask the references they have provided for other people they might know who have come into contact with the candidate.

» Depending on the reference policy of a company, the canned reference – 'I confirm xxx worked here from x to y' – could be considered a bad reference, or sour grapes. And if someone doesn't call back or is not available, then that can generally mean the candidate would not be top of their list either.

» Sales, now more than ever, is about credibility. Credibility needs to come from honesty. Once a salesperson becomes credible they earn the right to explore whether there is a deal. So this should come through in a recruitment process.

» Credibility is also the basis of authority, which establishes an organisation as an expert. A good interviewee establishes credibility with a recruiter and her colleagues. If someone isn't an experienced salesperson, but can establish credibility in an interview situation, then they are likely to make a good salesperson.

» Good salespeople will get those other than themselves to do all the talking – as will people who might make good salespeople.

» Good salespeople will establish themselves as a questioner and seek to make others answer their questions. They will *listen* carefully to the answers given and formulate new questions from them.

» Lastly, it is important that some tasks are set (see below) which a candidate needs to complete in order to demonstrate they are up to the job. These tasks need to be relevant and should test the candidates to demonstrate they are up to the mark.

It is important that a recruitment process has some fun in it while working out whether a candidate fits requirements. It is necessary to be persistent and have faith that the right person for a business will be found. The same goes for instincts; it is possible just to gel with someone who could be a major asset. Normally the right person will feel right very quickly.

PROJECTS & ACTIONS
QUESTIONS AND TASKS FOR
MANAGEMENT TO USE IN INTERVIEW

The following are divided into areas that an interviewer could consider important for a sales position:

• Money. You need to find out your candidate's attitude to money. For example: 'If I gave you £100,000 today, what would you do with it?' The answer to this can reveal a lot. If the interviewee says they would save it, invest it and generally keep it for a rainy day, they are more likely to be an account manager type. If they say they would spend it, they are more likely to be suited to getting new business. This could go either way with a business developer, but they may well say they would invest it.

Also, look out for whether they ask you about their ability to make money in the role you are offering – how that works and the detail. This is always a sensitive issue, but one that it is critical to get to as part of the sales process, so consider how they approach it. You should be prepared to discuss numbers, but place a limit on what will be discussed. Do they extract the information that you are prepared to give, or do they leave critical detail? Are they confident and skilled enough to bring up potentially delicate issues? Are they brash and pushy? Remember: getting a job with you is

continued

like finishing a deal, and this is how they are likely to act when working for you.

Ask them about meeting or beating targets, if that is applicable. You need concrete examples here; targets they can prove they actually met. Put the onus on them to provide proof, especially if there are big numbers or large amounts above the target. This shows whether they were either managed incorrectly and the targets were too low, or they really are that star performer.

- Listening. Testing proper listening is essential. One way to test this: while you are on a call or in an interview situation, drop some facts, numbers and details into the conversation. Then have a set of questions that asks the candidate to recall these, and see if they can.

- Empathy. You can find many free tools to test empathy on the Internet. Where possible, I like to adapt these and put in some of my own questions which are specific to the sales situation, to use in the hiring process (see www.salestribe.blog/empathy for a post with resources on empathy).

- Attitude. How do they come across? Desperate? Pushy? Brash? Nervous? See Chapter 1, Attitude and Approach, and phrase your questioning around these traits.

- Interests. Ask them about their interests. Maybe get them to write a list? Generally, what you are looking for is a broad range of interests, and the candidate's ability to talk about them with some passion and in some detail.

Ask them questions such as: 'Give me an example of the last time you went to that.' Or 'How often do you do that?' You are looking for them to actually show you that they have the domain knowledge. Get into the detail, make notes and dig as deeply as you can. People with broad interests generally engage much better with other people since they typically have something in common with a wider range of people. For example, most people have a favourite sport or sports team. Many people may play a musical instrument or like certain types of food. These can be quite emotional attachments which get a conversation going both well and quickly. Common interests also bridge age and peer-group gaps, in order to form the basis of relationships that might not have been possible before. Most importantly, common interests allow the salesperson to start to introduce *value* into the conversation since, with some domain knowledge, they should be able to offer a few recommendations. Lastly, in some cases, common interests help avoid 'hard-sell' situations which are only about the selling engagement.

- The above is not always true – buyers in organisations who know exactly what they are looking for will want to get straight to business and not engage in small talk. Knowing when to do the former and not the latter is also worth testing. In the first interview perhaps be open to chat and in the second cut straight to it?

- Analytical skills. Prepare some text which contains facts about a particular topic; not something that is public, something they might already have read, or even something with false data. It doesn't have to be about your company or industry, but it makes sense if it is. During your conversation – where you should expressly allow note taking – perhaps ask questions about why they may want to work for you. Drop in facts and certain things that you regard as potentially confidential and important to you, then ask them questions to find out how much of it has been retained/taken down, to see whether they were actually listening. Get them to build a picture back to you, with you asking questions and them talking.

- Remember that statistics are a salesperson's friend when it comes to building stories and credibility, so it is important that these are retained.

- Provide a fake set of numbers that may have come from a suspect or prospect. Ask them to analyse the numbers and present their findings back to you.

- Confidence. Ask them to give you five examples of when they found themselves outside their comfort zone. These can be in a business or personal context. When did these events take place? For the hunter-sales types they should be very recent, but can be longer term for business-development candidates. Account manager 'farmers' may struggle to reach five, or, typically, will provide very mundane examples.

continued

- Give the candidate a list of five suspects or prospects with whom you want them to set up a meeting for you. You can discuss the topic of conversation you want to have with the suspect or prospect, and allow them to ask questions in preparation. Tell them you are happy for them to represent you for this task. (If you have multiple candidates, do not give them the same list.)

- Persistence. This is vital for the hunters and the business developers. Ask them to give you some examples of their persistence and their results from it. Ask them how many times they would normally contact a suspect/prospect before making a decision about whether to stop. Is that it, or would there be a follow-up? What would trigger that? What attitude do they have about the suspect/prospect when they talk about them in this context? Is there a general attitude of building partnerships? You need concrete examples that they can prove to you. Dig deeply into this – be persistent!

- Presentation and demonstration skills. Test their presentation skills by making them pitch to you and your colleagues as if you were a customer for one of your products or services. Find out about their attitude to learning and demonstrating a product or service. Make it clear that this is considered an essential part of the job, and thus a requirement which will be associated with some measurement of performance.

- Numeracy skills. In all elements of sales activity numbers are important. Some people are naturally good with numbers, whereas others may have to work hard at them to make sure they are right. Either way, demonstrating recall and accuracy in handling them is important. Drop in numbers during your conversation and then test recall by asking about them. Ask about experience of modelling and showing numbers around deals. Who has done it before? Do they see this as their responsibility (as it should be)? Ask them to walk you through processes, with numbers around sales activities they have been involved in and that they have followed before. Can they show you examples? All candidates should be good here and be able to speak about numbers when they are answering questions and providing details of their career.

- Ask them to describe a business case that they have prepared, along with details and samples (without disclosing confidential information). Make sure you tell them that building a business case is important for the deals you want to close, to gauge reaction.

- Organisation and timing. Sales activity is about being organised. Ask a candidate what their day looks like, the typical processes they follow, software they have used and their ability to use other software (some are wedded to a particular CRM system, for example). You need to get some good examples and ask them to work out a way for you to check what they claim is accurate.

- Ask the candidate to write down what a typical day would look like to them. Then expand it to the weekly activities they would perform. How would they perform these activities? How much time is spent on the phone, in meetings, doing research, etc.? Get them to take you through it in detail.

- Methodologies. Ask your candidates to describe particular sales methodologies they have practised and how they work. Which books/blogs/resources have they digested on the subject of selling; which training courses have they been on? Get them to give an opinion about what might or might not work in your case.

- Targeting. Ask the candidate to explain how they would target a prospective customer for your business. How would they approach it? What support would they expect? Most people are looking for a self-starter who doesn't rely on others to provide 'leads' or rely totally on tenders or RFPs (Request for Proposal) for their approach.

  Confidence. As discussed in Chapter 1, Attitude and Approach, an essential component in the make-up of a good salesperson is a level of confidence. However, there are two types of confidence that a salesperson should possess. The hunters and business developers need personal confidence and the ability to handle rejection

continued

when things don't work out; they also need confidence to gauge whether a deal is going to work and either close it or move on.

Account managers need personal confidence to approach a situation with tact and diplomacy, and be able to deal with difficult and often complicated – both technically and emotionally – situations.

All these people need to have product-knowledge confidence that comes from being an expert in their field.

- Negotiation skills. Generally, all salespeople are going to have to negotiate in one way or another (see also Chapter 9, Finishing a Deal). This may be a simple process of agreeing a price but, more often these days, it is a longer process. This is a skill and it can require sensitivity and subtlety, as well as strong motivation. You need to build a picture of the level of negotiation you can expect from a person. If the sales role involves sensitive, confidential negotiation, which is increasingly common, you will need to cover this ground carefully, to give you the confidence that the person is able to perform this task. Ask questions about their experience, approach and tactics. It is surprising the number of organisations whose senior people are unable to negotiate.
- Finishing deals. This is coupled with the above, if applicable. It doesn't make sense to hire hunter-salespeople who can't finish deals, unless you know this upfront and just want them to open doors for you. This sounds crazy but you should make it clear that this is the focus from the beginning (which it should be!). Focus on questions around which deals they have previously closed. Focus on their quality and longevity. Are these customers included in the references provided? If not, why not?
- If this is the candidate's first role in sales, and you are taking on someone in the belief that they will be able to do this, ask them about getting things done in other areas of their life. You need to ask questions and gather evidence that the person is a doer; someone who will complete tasks following a process; a finisher – since that is what you are asking them to do for you.

- Education. This area is tricky. Some of the best salespeople have not been highly educated at all, at least in an academic sense. In fact this could be a secondary consideration to other topics in this list. Of course, it is important to check that the person has the qualifications they say they have. If they are well educated, it may well empower them and equip them well to engage, but a high-level or expensive education does not necessarily make someone credible, a good question listener or a problem solver.
- Network. It's not what you know, it's who you know. It is very easy to demonstrate an extensive network in certain software tools like LinkedIn and Facebook. If you set out to build a large network of people using these tools, then you can do so, but you will want some evidence as to the size and quality of a candidate's network.

  Ask them how they have developed their network and whether they have a strategy around who they connect with. Is their network relevant for your business? Who were the last people they connected with, and when was that? This should tell you whether this information is worth consideration or not. If you decide it is not, then consider asking for other evidence of network.
- Dealing with pressure. Salespeople are normally required to deal with crazy situations in one way or another: for instance, customers changing their minds on deals or negotiated terms; other members of their organisation complicating situations; people not doing what they say they will do – it can be a long list. Sales roles can be like herding cats. Ask questions on experience here and how they dealt with it. You are looking for a response that, where possible, doesn't include emotion. The problem here is that this is theoretical unless you test it, but ask the questions anyway.
- Languages. If you are interviewing someone who claims to speak a particular language or set of languages, then you need to check they can! This sounds obvious and basic, but people make claims and are not able to back them

continued

up. Suggestions would be to involve a local college or equivalent and ask them to have a conversation in the language required, or with customers or even an agency. For text, provide some business text that needs to be translated and can be checked.

- Account management/sales-based customer service. There is no reason why the test for this role cannot be one that is doing the actual job. Since this will mostly include a review of some business metrics, status of the relationship and perhaps pitching new products or services, this can be set as a test to complete with you and your colleagues in a staged situation, using false data.

3. Commission

Paying commission can be a powerful method for management to achieve sales goals for an organisation.

In this chapter we will discuss:
- Why pay commission?
- Carrot and stick: disincentives.
- Incentivising desired activity.
- Structuring commission.

Why pay commission?

Commission is often a real problem topic. Many people who run companies or are in management don't see why they would ever pay commission to certain people in their company but not to all of them. After all, everyone in the organisation works hard, don't they?

A lot of companies have bonus schemes that reward everyone with a share of some 'upside' at the end of a period, with a slice of a generated bonus pie rewarded to an employee on their merits, depending on how much they have gone beyond targets or responsibilities, for example.

So although companies can be run that way, and can expect the sales 'hunters' that bring it new business to perform in their jobs as others do, the expectation shouldn't be too high. And organisations which don't pay commission should not expect to have or to hire 'star performers'.

Commission for salespeople can have a dramatic effect on revenues and a sales individual's performance. One of the key traits of 'hunter-type' salespeople is that they are interested in making as much money as possible. If they are correctly targeted and shown the prize worth going for, they will endure significant stress and pressure to hit that target. Razor-sharp focus should come into play and it isn't unusual to be surprised at the obstacles they will overcome to get what is required.

A basic salary and a good commission plan in combination can work very well. But care should be taken that the base salary isn't too low to attract good people.

The problem with annual bonus schemes is that they don't necessarily correlate directly with the sales activity in question. People live in the here and now and don't take notice of longer-term benefits – especially salespeople, and especially if everyone else is getting the same bonus.

In Las Vegas, if one of the big jackpots is won, the winner is generally offered a choice: to take the amount won as payments over a period, at x amount per month, up to the actual amount won; or they are offered a lump-sum single payment that is much smaller than the jackpot that has been won, to be taken immediately. Overwhelmingly, most people opt for the lump sum over the payments since life is short and getting money now is a real reward.

Commission works because it correlates directly with the selling activity to influence behaviour immediately. It provides a win-win for both parties and a clear incentive for predefined activity. It is a powerful incentive.

Carrot and stick: disincentives

If commission is the carrot, consider also having a stick. An incentive is a great motivator, but disincentives are something worth considering so as to make sure things happen as anticipated. Consider levying some sort of penalty, such as a fine, if certain things are not done – for example, not keeping up with certain metrics, not making notes in meetings, and so on. These penalties can mean a lot and people will strive to avoid them more than may be considered, if they are structured properly. Especially if the individuals are 'named and shamed' as those penalised throughout the organisation – this can be much more of a motivation than the actual fine.

To be effective, disincentives need to be structured so that they are truly a penalty. Fining someone £100 if they are receiving a six-figure sum in compensation is unlikely to change their behaviour.

Disincentives are not meant to be used as a method of

bullying, but as a clearly communicated deterrent to avoid unwanted behaviour or actions.

Incentivising desired activity

It is imperative that the behaviour that is to trigger commission payments is worked out carefully. This sounds simple and obvious but most of the time it isn't worked through well, and this is where mistakes are made. If commission is paid to someone on just 'bringing a deal', then that is fine, but what does it mean? Considerations would be:

- What type of deal?
- What sort of revenue? Or profit?
- Is it a deal that has fulfilled x amount of the organisation's sales process? Which elements?
- Is it a deal with a certain type of customer?
- Does the commission apply to all deals and all customers in all markets?
- What sort of margin is there?
- Does it include existing customers or only new ones?
- And is that at the same rate of commission?
- Does commission only kick in when you hit a certain level of target?
- Or perhaps a group target?

It is important to be crystal-clear about what will be rewarded, how, and when the organisation will reward it. This should be agreed in writing and communicated clearly so it is understood by everyone concerned. Management should always reserve the right to change it at agreed times but should also always be prepared to pay what has been agreed. Delay, or don't pay, then commission becomes a disincentive, and salespeople will be very unhappy.

Structuring commission

For a sales 'hunter', it makes sense to pay a base salary that enables them to live a reasonable life, but then to reward them with a part of the revenues they are bringing in. This may enable them to double their salary if they hit the agreed target, and to make significantly more if they overachieve.

Commission can be based on revenue – or could be profit-related. Gross-margin targets can be introduced, so that no commission is paid if a certain amount of gross profit isn't made. This will incentivise the salesperson from giving away all the value of a deal in negotiations.

Some sort of percentage of banked or billed revenue or profit is often a fair reflection of the value the deal has brought to the company. If the revenue or profit received is to be generated as a service, or there is some kind of recurring-revenue stream, this percentage can potentially decrease over time to zero to incentivise new deals: for example, x per cent for year 1 of a deal, y per cent for year 2, and nothing thereafter.

The percentage rate can also be tiered upwards or

downwards depending on other factors, such as how a deal is structured, to provide further incentives. For example, the company may sell something where the customer pays some sort of fee on the signing of a deal and then a recurring service element over time. The margins may be very different to the company at different times of the deal's life, so it may be prepared only to share a higher percentage when the margin is better for the company in a revenue-based commission plan.

In addition, some cash is a good incentive on the signing of a deal. This focuses the salesperson on closing the deal and the end of the sales process. Finishing a deal needs focus.

Capping the commission or any incentive is possible but uncapped commission works well if it is clear, simple and rewards the desired behaviour – normally to finish more deals.

One way of limiting the commission paid is by creating some sort of specific bonus pool, which is generated from the overall profit and released every year/quarter/month. The salespeople will then work according to certain eligibility criteria, based on metrics (see Chapter 10), and then the amount should be apportioned based on their individual performance. Another way is simply capping it on each deal brought.

Commission should potentially be used to provide 'golden handcuffs' for those entitled to it. It can be layered by success in multiple deals; this way the best salespeople, the ones who sell more or larger (or both), will more likely be retained as they will want to enjoy the commission they have built up. And the underachievers leave because they are not successful and not bringing the company what it wants.

Account managers often respond to types of incentives other than money; for instance, holidays or other rewards, extra holidays, dinners, and so on, with partners or family, so they can demonstrate their success outside the company. This can make it more competitive and fun. Care should be taken over rewards which might carry the suggestion of forcing someone to do something with colleagues; most people don't want to spend time with their colleagues outside work unless they have to!

Recognising super-performance is often very successful. Some firms have a 'President's Club', a reward where the most successful person/people – measured in performance or even commission earned – can take their family on a luxury holiday in a very exclusive and highly publicised manner. This can create highly positive competition among salespeople.

Monitoring of these programmes over time is important. If they cease to be an incentive and are seen merely as an additional benefit that is rewarded regardless of achievement, they won't drive anticipated behaviours. They must be things that really appeal to those who are striving for the reward. For example, there is no point awarding a spa day to someone who wouldn't be seen dead at a spa.

The amount of commission and/or the likelihood of winning other incentives should be calculated easily and regularly so everyone knows where they are – at the end of each month, for example. Complicated commission plans shouldn't be used simply to hide nasty deductions that aren't communicated upfront.

PROJECTS & ACTIONS

- Write a list of what actions need to be incentivised for your business – what activity you want to bring through the incentives of a salesperson. Here are some things to think about:
    - What type of leads do you want generated and qualified? Do you want to reward ones that fit a specific profile differently based on the amount of work that has gone into them? Or on the complexity of the deal?
    - Will you have different commission structures for different products or types of deals? Or different types of salespeople?
    - Will more than one person get paid on a deal? The new business person who brought it and the account manager who will now look after it, for example. What are you comfortable paying?
    - Timing of payments – when will the commission be calculated, on what activity and when will it be paid? Will this be split into different types of payments that incentivise different things? For example, a cash payment on signing a deal and a share in the success of the deal over a particular period.
    - How long do you want a salesperson to 'own' the deal in its life – does this end when a contract is signed or an order is placed, or do you want them to have to own it through to delivery or longer? Do they get paid for subsequent deals?
    - Will you have a fixed target number that the salesperson will get paid if they achieve the targets set? Or will the salesperson share in what the company receives?
    - Is there a level of margin you need to achieve to pay levels of commission? Or a test of profitability for a deal which needs to be achieved? Are there 'pass-through' costs in your products that you won't pay commission on? For example, fees from a third party which mean that margin is low or zero.
    - If the targets are based on, for example, gross or net profits to the business, does that work and can it be calculated in a simple enough way which works for you?

Does this put confidential information on the business's performance into the public domain?

- Is what the company is offering meaningful enough to drive the behaviour that you want?
- How can management document it in as simple a way as possible but make it really clear what exactly is on the table?
- Does the commission plan provide for any element of 'lock-in' for the more successful people – i.e. they build up increasing commission over time that keeps them in the business.
- Who calculates, communicates and 'polices' the commission? Is there a management review and potential override process where discretionary payments can be made despite monetary performance – for example, if someone has worked very hard on a deal but it didn't happen or there are lots of orders but the company has been unable to deliver?

- Remember to provide a catch-all in the plan that allows you to pull out if necessary if a particular or unexpected behaviour comes to light and you don't want to pay commission for it. All payments are at management's discretion.
- Is commission payable after someone leaves the business or changes roles?
- How will management reward super-performance?
- For those other than salespeople, is there an incentive that can reward commercial activity, such as success in account management?

4. Becoming an Expert

Being seen as an expert source of information and knowledge in a market establishes and maintains credibility with potential buyers and existing customers.

In this chapter we will discuss:
- Characteristics of an expert.
- Components that make up expertise.
- How to get a company's expertise recognised.

Today's economy is increasingly founded on knowledge. What gives an organisation an edge is knowledge; knowledge about how things in their sector fundamentally work. The devil is always in the detail and can often mean the difference between success and failure. Customers need to see a whole organisation as a team of experts that has in-depth knowledge. An organisation they are compelled to engage with in order to stay ahead. A savvy organisation is all about having the knowledge – and knowing what to do with it – but also one that isn't afraid to learn as things change.

In a sales context, customers should be treated as experts whether they are or not. Customers react much more positively to being treated this way than to being lectured on how to do something. So it is important that they see a supplier and their staff as equals in their expertise, even if it is never discussed. It establishes credibility much more quickly in sales engagement, and it means that salespeople are empowered to ask the right questions to proceed through the sales process with a potential customer.

Characteristics of an expert

An expert is someone highly knowledgeable in a specific area, not a generalist. It is normally someone who has worked in that field for a relatively long period and who understands the finer detail of the subject matter, or is skilled in that area. An expert needs to be someone who is well versed in the practical details of the subject, and has considerable experience in 'actual' execution, rather than the 'theory' of execution.

An expert is not someone who has read a couple of articles in the industry press and then taken to social media to talk about it; or has only ever studied examples of how others have executed a particular project, plan, implementation of a service, and so on. They need to have done it themselves and got their hands dirty. There are a lot of faux experts today; many things are published authoritatively, but often the authors have only scratched the surface of the subject in which they are claiming to be experts.

The nuances of execution and the small things can really make a difference, and in a sales context this allows value to be added early in the process, so that it really means something to a prospective customer. The earlier value is added, the more likely the supplier will be able to uncover and solve the real problems and needs of a customer, which leads to finishing deals. It also helps support the demand for a realistic price.

Being an expert separates an organisation from the competition. It allows a company to establish a dialogue with prospective customers for reasons other than when they are just in buying mode, and potentially to be on their radar long before.

The goal here is to be one of the trusted sources of information in an industry or market sector; the first people that a prospective customer comes to if they want to know about a particular element of that market.

Components that make up expertise

We can split the knowledge that an expert needs into two parts, as it may take a long time to acquire it, and is generally an ongoing learning process in any living market. The first is product or service knowledge. The second is market knowledge. We explore both in more detail here:

Product or service knowledge

First and foremost, there should be a good knowledge of the product or service that the organisation is selling, and how it is positioned in the market to capture customers. There is no excuse not to have this knowledge as a sales professional. It is unacceptable for salespeople to say, 'Well, I'm not an expert on the technical details,' or 'I'm sure our product specialists can answer those questions for you.'

Of course, it is perfectly normal that mistakes can and will be made and that not every minute detail of a product or service is necessarily known, but in this age the salesperson needs to be a product/service expert insofar as is possible. They should know the ins and outs of the features and capabilities of the product, at least at the top level, and they should be able to talk with authority about it. They should also be able to back this up with knowledge of the business models and statistics that apply: how their product or service has affected the business of others. Naturally, it is fine to introduce other members of the team to talk about highly complex or technical elements, but the salesperson should lead the customer engagement and should be aware of why any conversation is taking place with the customer and how it fits the bigger picture.

Product or service knowledge needs to be backed by three further principles.

1. The first is that the salespeople themselves need to have some sort of legitimate interest in the product or service. There is no point trying to force a salesperson to be passionate about something they have no interest in, as this will come across when they talk to customers. If you are passionate about something, you are more likely to be a good advocate for it and also enjoy selling it!

2. The second is the willingness of the management of the organisation to help the salespeople learn about the product, and assist in any sampling activities so that the passion develops further. Training and immersion in the capabilities of an offering is essential. And the best staff should be assigned to support the salespeople, so they can develop a relationship with the people who actually deliver the product/service within an organisation. Then they can learn about how the products solve the needs of the customer to be able to understand what deals make sense.

3. Management should provide salespeople with any equipment they need to be able to show the product/ service in the best light. If they need a laptop with a super-screen and some special software on it to demonstrate the product, they should have these, and it is someone's responsibility to make sure it all works (along with the salesperson). If they need samples of a product, they should have access to them and it should be ensured that they are well presented. If they need to introduce prospects to customer-service people in the organisation who can talk about the service that is provided, then those people should know that and see it as part of their job to be available and to cooperate fully.

Market knowledge

In a connected business society market knowledge has become one of the most important characteristics of any organisation – and this is set to continue. Being seen as a leading knowledge-owner in a market has amazing value these days; this goes for a sales team and a company as a whole. To generate great conversations without having any 'hard sell', this should be a major focus. But it is important to look at what that actually means, because it involves more than just posting meaningless articles on social media that state the obvious. So how does an organisation keep up-to-date with its market so that it always has the best information?

Prospective customers and existing customers
Often the best information from the market is available by talking regularly to the people who are in it, and who are conducting business in the industry (we discuss this more fully in Chapter 8, on engaging with customers). It depends who is consulted, but there is little substitute for learning about markets in this way. Collecting this market intelligence is an important element of the sales function. It is vital that it is collected accurately, verified where possible, shared and used. It is important to be sensitive about confidential information: it must remain confidential, so ways need to be found of regurgitating some of that information, in an anonymous fashion, to use to an advantage. This should be an ongoing process. (There is a whole host of tools out there from simple, cloud-based notes applications to full-blown customer relationship management (CRM) systems.)

Press and PR
This area offers a greater amount of data in the Information Economy, where it was not necessarily available before. Organisations in most industries, their employees, associates

and trade groups are tripping over each other to put information into the market. Any organisation can capitalise on this but watch out for 'fake news'.

A strategy should be developed which identifies relevant news sources, and what is to be taken less seriously, so as to streamline the information intake. Otherwise it is very easy to spend a lot of time sifting through bland and meaningless information.

Every market has some sort of specialist trade press. The trade press used to be late in reporting some stories, but as information becomes increasingly free-flowing and the world seems to shrink, so the trade press has become much better informed – or at least faster at providing information to the market. A sales team should be well versed in what is happening, and generally it is free or cheap if done in the right way.

TIPS & NOTES

In one company it was one of our sales administrator's jobs to pull good information together from the various news sources and send a daily digest to our sales team. This digest didn't replace anyone's own reading, but was sent to lots of people across the organisation in many different departments, because it was done well and was valuable. This model could fit comfortably in an organisation's marketing function, and if you can scale that up to offer informed opinion alongside news articles, a valuable information source can be developed.

Public information

All public companies are obliged to issue regular investor relations pieces and reports. Some private companies issue these, too. For a small fee it is also possible to receive revenue and some structural information from Companies House on a company's filings to the government. Not only will reading offer an insight into the market trends and issues that are facing companies, but it will also provide a great view as to the challenges that the management of these companies are confronting. Understanding those issues and problems, whether or not a product or service fits that area completely, and having a good picture of the market will provide many benefits when it comes to engaging with a prospective customer. In many industries it is possible to subscribe to a service that will supply these updates and the analysis around them.

Most companies are proud of innovations in products or services and will issue press releases and papers explaining their innovations, trends and behaviours. These are often quite 'fluffy' as they are promotional pieces, but do sometimes include decent insights.

Conferences and exhibitions

There are usually lots of events in a market sector and perhaps the kindest thing to say is that they vary greatly.

Typically, it is difficult to gain much market intelligence at conferences that are focused on a particular market, unless the supplier is just starting out. Even on panels where there are senior and well-hardened CEOs of successful businesses, the individuals are highly unlikely to get up on stage and share their trade secrets.

There are always exceptions and a lot comes down to the quality of the event.

GET INSPIRED BY YOUR MARKET

One of the companies we built was in a sector where there was one major exhibition every year in the USA, at which all the big companies in the business used to launch their latest innovations. We didn't exhibit ourselves but we did attend; we would send a group of product experts from our development team who would walk the floor for four days, take photographs where they were able to and dig deep into anything they could. At the end of the trip they would write a report to the management and do a presentation to the whole company on what they had found: trends, market positioning and so on. Six months later they would do another presentation on how what they had found had influenced our product direction.

From a sales perspective, one large trade show (normally the same one each time) can be the place to find out about the competition, customer demands, pricing, rumours of mergers and acquisitions, and general gossip. Management should make sure the organisation takes comprehensive notes and that these are shared and acted upon.

A view from the end-customer

If the product or service is provided and the customer in turn uses it as part of a product or service offering to their customers, the team should really understand the perspective of the end-customer. The sales team should be able to talk about that consumer's behaviour with prospective customers, in order to uncover their needs. The salesperson should understand how an end-consumer engages with a prospective customer organisation and, wherever possible, 'be' an end-customer.

If the supplier organisation has lots of customers in a sector, the organisation should be able to examine the relationship with those customers and, without giving away confidential information, equip the salespeople with market knowledge that can be shared in the new business process and with existing customers.

Trends

A supplier organisation, and its sales team, should be able to offer educated opinions and back these up with real-world experience as to where the trends in the market are going. It should be versed in how customers' businesses will need to adapt or change to capitalise on market trends, or otherwise adjust their businesses to suit those trends. A supplier organisation should be willing to support those changes through its product or service, and show a clear vision of how these enhancements can be executed. It is not uncommon to see pieces ghost-written by CEOs and published to a mailing list, or to social media, that just don't say anything at all. If a supplier organisation publishes something, it needs to be relevant and provide some unique insight. This is an area where quality should come before frequency.

Competition

In *The Godfather Part II*, Michael Corleone says, 'Keep

your friends close, but your enemies closer.' These are very wise words for salespeople. A sales organisation should build a picture of the competition, and continually verify it wherever possible. It will empower them in many ways and influence how an organisation approaches deal-making.

One strong rule should be observed about competition – a competing supplier's organisation should never bad-mouth them. It looks terrible and actually helps the competition in any deal-making situation. They may have strengths and it is a salesperson's job to know about weaknesses. Instead of shouting out the shortcomings from the rooftops, it is much better to empower the prospective customers to expose those weaknesses. This is achieved by pointing them in the right direction and focusing on a supplier's strengths over those weaknesses.

It is a good strategy to know competition well. Good salespeople will know them personally and develop a relationship if possible. There will normally be many benefits without discussing sensitive information. If ways can be explored of working together, as a trade group of some influence over others, for example, it can often lead to better knowledge of the competition.

People knowledge

The people an organisation knows, the positions they fill and the colleagues they may have can be unexpectedly important. A salesperson's network and the way people treat them count hugely towards their status as an expert.

If an organisation is an expert in a market, it will know how that market fits together. If customers are known well, the people who work within the customer's organisation will also be known and, over time, they will reveal their strengths and weaknesses. A supplier's organisation will have established a confidential exchange of information. For example, it shouldn't be a surprise when customers or prospective customers ask for a recommendation regarding who they should hire (or maybe fire!). Good salespeople should know who the best people are in their market because they should be talking to everyone in that market.

The more a salesperson helps individuals in this context, the more kudos and robust relationships are developed. Obviously, recommending that someone poach an important customer's staff is possibly problematic. But if great people are working in an organisation and are not a customer or likely to be one, it is a great way of supporting a prospective customer's needs, while also potentially hurting the competition.

PROJECTS & ACTIONS

- What makes your organisation a group of experts? Establish a list of things that you can put across now which gives your organisation a unique perspective on the market, service or product area in which you operate. How is this valuable to your prospective and existing customers?
- How does your organisation capture and share knowledge in each of the sectors described above? How does it use that knowledge to influence its approach to the market?
- Develop some statistics or even statistical models that can support your opinions. Make sure they are well grounded.

How to get a company's expertise recognised

How does an organisation use knowledge in a way that is meaningful to its sales efforts?

The first principle should be less is more, both in terms of quantity of information and potential activity. Any activity should be relevant, truly meaningful and valuable to the prospects; punchy and current. Where possible, it should be something that others aren't doing, or offer a perspective that is somehow different or controversial. There should be an assertion of authority over a subject to give it credibility. For example, setting up a Twitter feed which publishes information every forty-eight hours because it seems like the right thing to do may well not be the right approach. When something is released, people need to want to digest it.

The second principle is, wherever possible, only to give the information to the people who find it valuable, rather than pushing it around to the widest possible audience. It should be used to target the potential customers who fit the ideal customer profile discussed in Chapter 5, or existing customers.

A website

It sounds obvious, but a supplier's website should be the primary source of information for people who want to find out about the subject in which they are experts. It is most likely that someone will read about a topic, trend or a market and then arrive at the website through an Internet search before reading the material. If the material is sensitive and presenting it openly is a problem, there are lots of ways of giving basic information and generating contact from a website or using a registration process to start a dialogue with a prospective customer. These days it is possible to track and analyse all activity and even link it to a CRM system to allow proactive contact of a prospective customer or much deeper knowledge of what a prospective customer is interested in when they make contact using artificial intelligence (AI). A social media presence should support the traffic generation to a website in as optimised a way as possible.

Workshops, events and presentations

A great way that can work exceptionally well, for both small and large companies, is to host prospective customers in a thought-leading event. Obviously, this has to be based around a subject which prospective customers are interested in, generally has to be free and should be well targeted. It needs to avoid being a hard sell, which will make people feel uncomfortable, but can obviously help capture certain information. Face-to-face engagement is always best, but it can also work through Internet-based tools, provided it is handled carefully. Having even a small number of people from a prospective customer organisation attend an event can work well.

There has to be something interesting to say – not just a monotonous sales pitch, although a small sales pitch can be part of it. It needs to add real value, perhaps something they can take with them and use. Maybe a paper or something informative to take away can be offered, which helps cement a supplier's credibility, or offer some sort of discount or trial for a product or service?

The objective is to establish a company as a bunch of experts and not a hard sell. A secondary objective should be to learn as much about the prospects and their business, status and so on. This is why face-to-face interaction is often much better since it is still difficult to have a meaningful conversation virtually, where the questions needed to uncover the requirements of a customer can be asked, but that is not impossible.

The salespeople should run the event and work the follow-up, but the presentation doesn't necessarily need to be conducted by them.

Get on the conference and press circuit

Another effect of the boom in information is that in most industry sectors there can be one event per day that an organisation could attend, or perhaps even speak at. It could be difficult to establish an organisation as experts if representatives attend all the events and repeatedly say the same thing. It is much better to pick one or two events that are well researched and can be targeted as well attended by people matching an ideal customer profile (see Chapter 5). These events should also be attended by the most senior people in the market, which may involve some sort of sponsorship or financial participation in the event.

If events are picked wisely, and any contribution delivers something of value (while also delivering a sales pitch), it should yield prospective customers.

It is also a good idea to offer interviews to the trade press or other media outlets where a similar message is delivered.

Press people will usually claim that editorials and advertising are not linked, but that is often not the case. Any advertising that is required in a specific place at a specific time should be expected to be paid for. This should be carefully selected and consideration should be given as to whether or not it is worthwhile – if a seller organisation knows who its customers are, it is already paying the sales team to engage with them.

Blogging and social media

Blogging is good for sales. It should be a primary activity which feeds other company information sources. How often a company chooses to blog is something that needs to be determined, but it should support the sales message and provide more ammunition to establish a company's expertise in the market. Like all the other methods, blog posts should have authority, deliver something of value and be used as primary communicators in all social media channels. The content should typically come from a number of places in the organisation, but it is a normally a function of the marketing department to develop and publish them. The salespeople can then use them as leverage in their targeting.

Obviously blogging can cover a wide variety of topics but should not divulge any confidential information or business strategies, tactics, etc.

Conversations with prospective and existing customers

This is explored in further detail in Chapter 8, Engage, but the places where the most impact is probably made are in meetings, during phone calls and when generally engaged with customers. Any organisation's team should be capable of demonstrating their expertise in these situations and asking the right questions (Chapter 7, The Sales Process) that develop customers' needs and thinking.

Fake it till you make it

What if the business is just starting up and it's too early to present it as a credible expert in the market? After all, in such a disrupted world it is quite possible that an organisation can be breaking new ground and not know a lot about an industry. The answer is to find someone who does. One benefit of the gig economy is that there are plenty of people out there who can offer expertise, and aligning with them can teach relevant personnel and help establish a company as experts at the same time.

Perform a high-profile industry product launch at an event

Select an event, such as a quality trade show or conference, where the list of attendees is likely to be the demographic of an ideal customer. Pick out or develop a new feature to a product or service. It doesn't need to be that innovative or creative, but it does need to be new and to be presented as something that has game-changing characteristics. Create an air of mystery around it by keeping it secret and promoting the launch. Launch it to a fanfare at the event to which all have been invited. Make sure that while attendees are watching the launch they are captured by the sales team and lots of other authoritative information is available. As with all events, follow-up is critical.

PROJECTS & ACTIONS

- Develop a list of channels that suit your company with regard to how you will put this information into the market. Who has primary responsibility for this in your organisation? How do your salespeople make the most of this information?
- Decide how frequently you would like to put information out into the market. Perhaps set up a calendar with an annual schedule of activity triggered by specific events so you can plan well in advance.

---

5. An Ideal Customer Profile

Before targeting an organisation to become a customer, it is important for management to understand what sort of customers the seller's organisation is looking for. If there is more than one sector, then this exercise should be completed for each.

In this chapter we will discuss:
- An ideal customer profile and what to do with it.
- Considerations that make up an ideal customer profile.

An ideal customer profile and what to do with it

This is a critical first phase in the sales process (Chapter 7). Collecting this information is what identifies a lead, cold connection – or a *suspect* – and works out or qualifies them as becoming a *prospect*. Once they have qualified as a prospect, going through a supplier's sales process with them may make them a customer.

Before starting targeting or marketing, it is important to understand what an ideal customer may look like. Even if there are not yet any customers for a business, assumptions should be made. To get the best out of this process, adapt the questions below to make sure the profile is being honed over time.

The world is changing so quickly now that most supplier organisations need to adapt their approach as they receive new information. A supplier organisation should always be focused on attracting the best customers for a business. All businesses need to change as they grow (or contract). All parts of the company that are involved in delivering the product or service should be represented in this process, not just sales.

The Information Economy has helped make a lot of information more easily available, but it is still a task of the sales function (or pre-sales/marketing) to collect the relevant information and verify it against the list of criteria that has been developed. There are some tools that help do this (see www.salestribe.blog/list-generation), but care should be taken that the information they reflect is accurate.

If the information cannot be found through public sources, connections should be used to work up assumptions. A well-networked individual may be able to discover this information anecdotally from piecing together information from others and using experience, but a match to the ideal customer profile should always be confirmed with the prospective customer as they go through the sales process.

It is the job of a supplier's sales function to perform this task. If a supplier's suspects and prospects are unwilling to share this information, salespeople will need to piece it together carefully over time and must treat it as confidential. Ultimately, if getting the information required to convert them from a suspect or prospect proves too painful, consideration should be made as to whether or not the prospective customer is worth pursuing at all.

PROJECTS & ACTIONS
CONSIDERATIONS THAT MAKE UP
AN IDEAL CUSTOMER PROFILE

Two things make up the profile of your ideal customer; try to develop a list of questions around them. The first is demographic considerations and the second is psychographic and behavioural considerations.

1. Demographic considerations

These are generally concrete things: the things that people often put on their website, social media, trade press or in news releases, or, if they are a public company, in their annual report. They are tangible and normally a measurable, factual piece of information.

Make a list of what you want/need to know. Here are some considerations to get the process started:

- Consider their overall revenue/profit/earnings before interest, taxes, depreciation and amortization (EBITDA). How big are they? Is that relevant?
- Revenue/profit/EBITDA in your sector. If it is not their core business, how big is the bit which is being targeted versus the overall business? Is it a profitable organisation/business unit?
- Debt. Do they owe money? Are they able to service the debt? Will that affect a relationship with a supplier's company?
- Shareholders. Are there particular shareholders or individuals involved with an ideal customer who are a

continued

problem to work with? Are there particular shareholders who won't work with the supplier?

- Age of company; age of people who work in it. The beginnings of an ethical and cultural fit?
- History. Start-up, small-/medium-sized business, large company, private/public company, government?
- Geography. Where is an ideal customer doing business now? Offshore/onshore?
- What markets are an ideal customer in? How important is each market to them?
- What sort of systems/technology/infrastructure do they operate? Does it need to be a particular make or manufacturer to work with a product or service?
- How many employees do they have? How many in the relevant sector?
- What sort of raw resources does the ideal customer have in order to execute a project in the area?
- What does the management team look like? Who would be a target?
- Is there a route to target through an existing network/ customer referrals?
- Is there a management function that is responsible directly for the target part of the business? What does that role look like – is it likely to have one or many different job titles?
- Is the sector seen as a growth/contracting area for your ideal customer?
- What industry trends/challenges are they dealing with in the markets they target?
- What top three needs (see Chapter 7, The Sales Process) they possibly have that can be solved in a demographic context?
- What headline piece of information would attract their attention and make them start to recognise the supplier as experts? How would that be backed up with a broader conversation?
- Is there a particular strategic partner necessary to get through to them?

- Do they have a marketing budget which can support the product on offer?

And so on. This list can be as short or as long as you want it to be, but generally (and as here) about twenty honed and razor-sharp points work well.

2. Psychographic and behavioural considerations

These are generally the intangible, immeasurable things: the things that can't be discovered normally and accurately from anything other than engaging with the customer over time and working them through, such as culture, ethics, diversity and inclusion practices. If there are demographic but no psychographic considerations, only a partial picture of the customer will be available to the salesperson. Psychographic details are not generally public and that can have real value for the supplier.

Here are some suggestions for these:

- What needs does an ideal customer have that can be fixed by the supplier organisation? What questions is it necessary to ask to find out?
- What access will an ideal customer need to give to the supplier for it to have access to the right people and resources to execute a successful project?
- What is an ideal customer company culture like? How much does it need a match with the supplier culture?
- An ideal customer will have no problem going through a sales process. Specifically, they will answer questions generated by the sales process (Chapter 7).
- Are the demographic considerations collected before there was an engagement actually correct? Do they still match the ideal customer profile?
- Have they spent, or are they spending, money on a product or service like this before?
- What do they say about their current supplier? What does an ideal customer say about their current supplier?
- If this sector is a new business area for the customer, how seriously are they taking it emotionally? This is not about the demographic situation. This is more about the attitude

continued

individuals in the customer organisation have regarding a new sector they may be entering. Are they bullish, excited?

- What is happening in their market from the perspective of an ideal customer (not from the numbers)?
- What sort of investment is necessary for the supplier to provide them with what they need?
- What outside influences should be avoided that are not controlled by an ideal customer? Which may scupper a successful project: regulators, trade bodies, emotional shareholders etc.?
- Does an ideal customer need to have licensing deals with other people to use a product or service? Are they prepared to do this?
- Do they need a business plan that will be shared with the supplier? What happens if they don't have one, or do have one but won't share it?

It may seem as if some of these are unnecessary for some businesses, so they should be scaled up or down as required. An ideal customer needs to fit a supplier, since bringing deals with these customers should be the ultimate target of the salespeople in a supplier organisation.

Asking questions that are necessary to build the profile shouldn't be something that a salesperson is afraid to do, but they should be realistic. Doing so at the beginning saves time and potentially signing deals with a difficult customer that is a problem to service or where a product doesn't fit.

6. Pricing

Pricing is one of the most important parts of doing business with others: it is a fundamental piece of the puzzle that can significantly contribute to (or detract from) revenue; it is one of the major things that can be changed to make a difference; it is also one of the most complex.

The Information Economy means that, whether it is desirable or not, a supplier's pricing is going to become increasingly public and available to its customers, its competition and to others it may not want to have it. A supplier's management must have clear reasons why it charges what it does for a product or service, and must bolster raw pricing with value-added elements, so it is not the single issue on the negotiating table.

In this chapter we will discuss:
- What is something worth?
- Value.
- De-risking and determining the price.
- Everyone loves a discount.
- Defensible pricing.
- Being too cheap.

- 'Most-Favoured Nations' and similar value killers.
- Simple or complicated pricing?
- When to introduce pricing.

TIPS & NOTES

One thing is for sure: you can always reduce your price, but it is almost impossible to increase it once it is out there!

What is something worth?

Just because someone says something is worth x doesn't mean it is; just because a price is published for a product or service doesn't mean that someone will actually pay that price; and just because one company or person pays a price for a product or service doesn't mean that it will command that pricing from all other customers. A product or service is only worth the amount someone actually pays for it. Management needs to decide what sort of supplier they are, and this will determine how they address their pricing, with two fundamentally different approaches:

1. Always sell at the lowest price possible, hoping to outcompete competitors and try and deliver just enough to maintain a margin.

2. Add enough value to the products and services offered so that it is considered a premium product. Develop relationships with customers who are willing to pay for good quality at a price they understand is more expensive than they may find elsewhere, but which delivers value they

recognise is difficult to find elsewhere. Don't take forward customers who just want the lowest price, regardless of quality or value.

Fundamentally, both of the above are subject to the same outside pressures in terms of competition on pricing; both will probably need some sort of justification, even as part of a well-honed sales process; and both will have challenges. It is possible to go with the first approach above and 'buy' the customer and then try and eke out additional profitability as a relationship develops, but there are risks associated with that.

But which one delivers better customers for a business? Which one builds loyalty and provides a reason other than price for people to be a customer? Which one determines what something is really worth, by including all elements for consideration, not just a final figure?

Value

For more complex deals, those that require longer engagement with a prospective customer, and more sales expertise in the Information Age, it isn't possible to discuss price without talking about value. Value is a primary reason why someone will pay a price for something. A lot is said about how things should have 'value': people talk about the sales process 'having a value'; about engagement with a company 'having a value'. But what does this really mean?

The word 'value' has been cheapened somewhat by certain retail organisations using it to mean 'cheap'. 'Cheap' is a negative word; 'value' should be a positive one. It's not a good idea to use the word 'value' in communications, but it should be at the forefront of the mind of management in terms of what is being delivered, and a key measure both internally and externally.

It shouldn't be difficult to examine all the areas where a company adds value in a customer relationship: both tangible (clear and definite) and intangible (vague and abstract); things that are the responsibility of a supplier to provide – and this should become an area of differentiation.

A supplier should consider:
• Their expertise and ability to deliver.
• The equipment they provide.
• The components/materials that make up their products and/or services.
• The way they manufacture.
• The reliability of a service and commitments that are being made around it.
• The people it employs and their ethics, attitude and approach.

The list can be extensive and is normally a combination of several items that can be focused on as areas of excellence.

If a supplier or individual salesperson is receiving price objections from a customer when they are in buying mode, the sales function is probably not doing a good enough job of creating value in the sales process. Creating value in the sales process is all about asking the right questions to find the needs of the customer that can be fixed by the supplier.

TIPS & NOTES

Smaller sales, or sales that can be completed in a short engagement with a prospective customer, are more influenced in pricing by the features and benefits offered. 'The X450 has more features than the X350 and so is £50 more expensive.' Buyers in the Information Age most likely already have these facts when they engage with a supplier.

If a supplier's aim is achieved correctly, management will set up its organisation and sales processes to deliver the greatest amount of value it can in all phases of engagement with a customer. Value in each of these areas:

• *Value before* a supplier enters a sales process with a customer, it will establish itself as an expert in the field: it will be a crutch for any prospective customers to lean on for industry information and guidance in that field, to ensure they are making informed decisions. For those customers who already consider themselves experts in their market, the supplier will seek to offer validation for their expertise and make it easier to buy.

TIPS & NOTES

As we discussed in Chapter 4, Becoming an Expert, the goal here is to be the first, or one of the most trusted and informed, sources of information. Your sales function, along with marketing elements such as your website, blog, etc., will be the point where this expertise begins to be delivered

---

continued

to the market and feedback is gained, but your whole company will be able to contribute to this. This should have value whether the prospective customer chooses to do business with you or not, but should not give away the key assets or reasons to work with you that can be recreated by your competition.

- *Value while* the supplier and customer are in the sales process. The sales process should normally start by establishing a confidential environment where the prospective customer and supplier organisations are able to engage and share information over time – a process that works out whether it is right to do business together. It's a bit like building a business plan. The supplier should make sure that it holds value for the prospect, whether there is an appetite to go forward with the deal or not. It can empower their thinking around a project or need and help them get what is right for them. Normally, this hinges on asking the right questions to establish what the true needs of a customer are before presenting solutions to those needs.

- *Value after* the sales process and once the customer has an existing relationship with the supplier's organisation. This is perhaps where the most value can be brought to bear for the customer. If the sales process has been followed, and the job of engaging the new customer has been executed through delivery of projects and products that are part of the engagement, the customer should already be experiencing, and continuing to experience, good value from a supplier organisation, supported by the account management functions in that business.

It is important there is focus on these three distinct areas – before, during and after the sales process. Measuring the success of each should be made an ongoing project and someone in the supplier's organisation should ideally be responsible for monitoring and measuring them.

Of course, there is another factor in value and that is the historical picture of where the customer has come from, and the products/services and service levels they may have received in the past from other providers. If they are already paying a significant premium over the price a new supplier is able to offer, then offering it cheaper has headline value.

Adding value through strategic relationships

Consider that, as experts in your markets, you may have an edge to offer a customer over a pure product or service on a broader level. An example of this would be an offer of some financial investment or expertise from a team of qualified individuals, along with a deal that allows a supplier to lock out the competition and make a true strategic partnership with a customer. This should be carefully considered since providing this for one customer may alienate another.

PROJECTS & ACTIONS

- List all the areas in your business that currently add value to customer relationships outside of price.
- Then list all of the things that you could do to add further value. Mark which of these are unique to your organisation in your market, over the competition. Hopefully you will end up with a list of at least ten major things and a bunch of small

---

continued

> things that you should be communicating in a sale which differentiate you from the competition above purely price.
> - List ten questions you can ask a customer that will help you to communicate that value to them.

De-Risking and Determining the Price

A supplier should be proud of its pricing if it truly adds the value it believes it does. If it is continually striving to be an expert in a market, and constantly solving the problems and needs of customers, it should be able to stand behind its pricing. But a supplier should also consider being able to provide innovative business models that work for a customer to de-risk its pricing to the buyer, even at a premium level. This is becoming more and more common in the Information Age because it suits recurring fee business models greatly but, with a bit of creativity, it can be applied to other business models.

Examining barriers to doing business with a supplier's organisation and how its competition charges is a constant and important task, but also a good way to explore de-risking the pricing. Consider:

- If the competition charges big initial fees and demands upfront financial commitments, then can an innovative supplier offer the opposite?
- If the competition demands high hourly or daily rates, can that be switched around so something more flexible is offered to make it more palatable, but ultimately supports the supplier's pricing?

Pricing

- If the competition demand long-term contracts which tie the customer up, a supplier may consider offering a rolling contract that enables the customer to serve notice on short terms – if a supplier is delivering value, there is often no way the customer will look to go anywhere else, regardless of the term that is in the contract.
- A supplier may offer an option to cap the value of a project at something fair so the customer has certainty around it without ending up losing money.
- If the product or service has a low enough cost of delivery, the supplier may offer the opportunity for the potential customer to start using the product or service at no cost, but with some commitment that the cost will be applied after a period. This concept is being adopted by many technology companies.

Finding the place to innovate in the way a business is established with a customer will help support a premium pricing structure, and de-risk it for the individuals in the customer's organisation. De-risking the pricing can mean there is no need for negotiation – it makes it easier for customers to buy.

Determining the price

'Race-to-the-bottom' pricing wars are common in saturated markets where products and services have become a commodity, and everyone is adding the same or no value. If someone decides to drop, everyone else follows. Once pricing becomes the only point of differentiation it only works to the benefit of the customer and then often only in the short term. In the Information Age, this happens more quickly.

Intelligent customers should understand that they need their suppliers to make money in order to be able to provide them with quality products or services. That their suppliers are part of an ecosystem they have a responsibility to protect in order to continue to receive good service or quality products.

Despite the above, people will want to pay the cheapest price they can for what they are able to get. It's human nature. No one wants to pay the most, or to feel as if they are.

The only real way to find a 'true market value' for anything is likely to be an auction, where a starting price is set and customers – who in this scenario would all have identical business models and identical ways to engage with you and to use your product or service – are asked to bid to determine the 'fair market price'.

Of course, this is the sort of thing that may be suggested in a theoretical textbook by people who haven't really done it. In the real world a supplier needs to try and set fair pricing around its business and how it works, then may need to have the flexibility to massage it to find the right level in each situation, based on individual customer's situations.

Taking value into account, there are three factors that need to be considered to determine pricing:

1. Profitability.
2. Competition.
3. Customers.

1. Profitability

Margin should be calculated carefully for each product or service, even approximately, before any pricing is set.

- Knowing the difference between what a product sells for and what it costs to make it, supply or deliver it is essential.
- For example, if a price is set at 100 and it costs 20 to make a product and 120 to deliver it and make it work for a customer, no money will be made.
- Set a price below which most deals will be rejected, unless in exceptional circumstances, or don't accept any negotiation on the price that is set.
- Or if it works better, a target margin floor can be established for each product set.
- Margin should not be communicated widely, especially not to salespeople, since there is a risk that all deals will be done at the bottom level. Margin is certainly something that should be protected from reaching a customer where possible.
- Consider tying commission to a level of profitability on deals.
- Suprisingly, some companies do deals at prices without fully understanding whether they will make money from them or not.

2. Competition

'Competitive pricing' is just another way of saying 'cheaper' – that is, cheap compared to the competition.

- Wherever possible, what the competition charges and what is being delivered for that price should be known intimately.

- What the competition delivers means not only the product or service, but also all the value, as discussed above. Knowing one without the other is all but worthless, primarily because, without that knowledge, it is impossible to compete without selling purely on price.
- It is rare that any product or service is identical. If it is, then it is something that will be commoditised rapidly in any sizeable market, and pricing will need to be at flat market rates to compete – there may as well be an auction.
- A supplier in a competitive market, which is adding and communicating true value and striving to deliver a quality product or service, shouldn't be the most expensive. Somewhere between the middle and the highest is often an optimal position.
- A customer who wants to beat a supplier to the ground on pricing either isn't understanding the value that a supplier brings – the ability for a supplier to solve its problems and fulfil its needs – or just wants the cheapest price regardless of circumstances. It may not be worth dealing with the customer at all – a true mismatch.

3. Customers

Buyers may well tell a seller the price they will pay for something. They may offer detailed information from others in the market.

- Make sure this information is constantly collected and verified in detail.
- A supplier's existing customers may also be a source of information on offers they are getting from competitors,

depending on the relationship between them and their supplier.

- Sometimes, it is healthy for a supplier to be asked by prospective customers, and even existing customers, to drop a price in order to win a deal. The proviso is that the customer is well informed, is comparing one thing with another correctly *and* the salesperson has a track record of uncovering needs and building value to fulfil those needs. This can be an indication that the supplier's pricing is finding market value.

- Pricing feedback from existing or prospective customers should have a mechanism for consideration within the supplier organisation. Don't be afraid of the conversation – better to have it than to not know it!

PROJECTS & ACTIONS

- Work out your gross margin for each product or service you provide. Is it high enough to allow you to make money?
- Does your pricing provide flexibility to give away margin in order to be competitive?
- Set that rock-bottom pricing now, but don't communicate it widely. Don't deviate from it, even if the big deal comes!
- How cheap are you versus your competition? Is that necessary? Are you somewhere between the highest and the mid-range pricing on the market? If not, why aren't you? How do you get there?

SHOPPING ON PRICE ALONE

We had a prospective customer who was in the market for one of our products – a technology that would be the foundation of a new part of their existing business offering. They were well positioned and the opportunity could become a serious business for them if they did it properly.

The stakeholders from this organisation talked about pricing before they had fully understood what they were buying or the needs they had to satisfy and problems they would have to solve. They placed a lot of emphasis on pricing without considering what needed to be done to deliver the best for the project, or the value in the proper implementation of it.

These guys were fantastic, and we had a lot of fun presenting our products and services to them. Our personal and professional relationships were excellent. The product would have given them what they needed in the time frame they were looking for to launch the service on the market, and to start making them money.

We could add a lot of value over our competition by advising them on best practices since we had other customers in the region doing the same. There were some complicated elements in the project but nothing we couldn't overcome. We could save them a lot of pain. Both parties seemed keen to do a deal.

After a few weeks of further conversations, they informed us that they would be choosing a competitor over us. That competitor claimed they could deliver all that we could and more (even though we knew that wasn't the case), but their pricing was massively different from ours.

We ran our numbers and explained to them that we didn't see how the competitor could afford to deliver the product at the price they were quoting, and that it might mean that their project would be given low priority in the competitor's organisation and that they would, therefore, probably not hit their deadlines and be late to the market with their project. This, in turn, would mean their competitors would be on the market before them and be taking their customers from them. But they still chose to go with our competitor, purely on the basis of price.

A year and a half later, after our salesperson had been in regular contact, they came to see us again.

The competitor had indeed not been able to deliver to their expectations. Nor did it seem that they ever would be. The customer was over a year late with their project and still had no offering on the market. They were quite desperate, and some people were in danger of losing their jobs. They now fully appreciated the difference.

It didn't mean they didn't still want a good deal and we had to move some on our price, but this time we struck a deal. Overall, we had stuck to our principles, kept a respectable margin and in the end got a deal that was good for both companies.

Everyone loves a discount

It doesn't matter if it is a buy-one-get-one-free offer, a certain percentage reduction or a straight, 'I am giving you x off because you are you': everyone loves some sort of discount or offer that suits their needs. A smart supplier will plan for this wherever possible. It can be used in a time-based way to get a deal over the line, as leverage to get better payment terms, or to sweeten the offer after a hard negotiation. A discount makes people think they have got something special. It should be made to appear personal to the customer wherever possible.

Defensible pricing

An important factor for most businesses in the modern era is how pricing travels. The world is getting smaller, information travels faster and the economy is moving towards a freelance economy, where people don't have specific full-time jobs but contract for certain skills in one industry or several. As people move around, pricing will inevitably travel with them – it doesn't matter how many confidentiality agreements have been signed. It is critical, therefore, that a supplier has a pricing model that is defensible to its customers. If a particular customer has a better price than similar customers a supplier works with, it may well only be a matter of time before the same pricing will be required by other customers. A supplier should potentially consider how it would be able to justify its pricing if its books were open to all its customers.

Being too cheap

This can be a problem area for start-up companies, and sometimes with new product introductions from larger companies. It is obviously a great thing to go out and get customers for a new product or service, and it makes sense to offer a good price when launching or to attract new customers, but the message this gives should be considered carefully.

Larger companies, or companies that use similar products or services to those that are being introduced, will already have suppliers and they will be used to a certain level of pricing (normally one of the items on a salesperson's list of questions, if they don't know it already). There is a risk that buyers won't take a supplier seriously if the price of the product or service is too low. Being able to offer the same or better product/service and still make good margin from it at a lower price may be irrelevant; low pricing may negatively affect a supplier's credibility.

SOMETIMES EXPENSIVE IS GOOD

I am a keen wine drinker. A few years back when I lived in California, my father, also a wine drinker, came to visit and we decided to go to Napa Valley to tour some vineyards. At the end of one of the tours we tasted some wine. The host informed us that one was a bottle of wine that was priced at $125. We tasted it and it was OK, but nothing special – equivalent to something you would pay significantly less for in Europe, perhaps even two or three times less. We chatted to our host and asked him about it. His quiet *response was that in the preceding few years they had been able to triple the price of the wine and it had actually helped sell it by it being more expensive. The same wine at a cheaper price wouldn't have sold nearly as well. Customers perceived it to be better because it was more expensive.*

Who should set the price?

There should be a clear understanding across the organisation of who is responsible for setting and agreeing the pricing of products and services. Many companies these days deliver complicated projects which involve services or products that need some sort of integration, not just technically, but with the people in an organisation. Typically, there are many people who perform this work across a supplier organisation. The pricing of a project or service, however, and whether or not something is 'going to make money', should be left to designated people and their interface with senior management of the company. Wherever possible, unstructured challenges by project managers, implementation teams, lawyers, accountants, and so on, should be avoided or a supplier's staff can become its own competitor in engagement with the customer.

'Most-favoured nations' and similar value killers

Following the Second World War, in 1947, an organisation called the General Agreement on Tariffs and Trade (GATT) was established. It existed until 1995 under this name, when it became the World Trade Organization (WTO). Its role is to 'provide a forum for negotiating agreements aimed at reducing obstacles to international trade and ensuring a level playing field for all, thus contributing to economic growth and development'. One of its fundamental principles is 'trade without discrimination', and part of this is the principle of 'Most-Favoured Nations' (MFN). In simple terms, this means that everyone is treated equally and, on the level of the WTO, it means that countries cannot normally discriminate between their trading partners in order to provide more favourable terms to one party over another – such as lower customs duty, for example.

In commercial agreements, the principle is that, with an agreed MFN, a supplier for one customer won't ordinarily be able to offer better terms to another for the same products and services without offering the same terms to the existing customer. The way it is implemented is normally an undertaking as part of a legal agreement: that no other customer will receive better commercial terms than the customer adopting the agreement, and, if they do, the supplier will either match those commercial terms or offer some other remedies.

The problems with this are many, primarily because if a supplier is providing solutions which address needs and problems a customer is facing, and they are adding value working with the customer, then guaranteeing that each customer gets the same commercial deal is difficult. If a supplier's business or industry is growing, often what may seem like fair pricing across the board can quickly become outdated – especially in the aftermath of customer mergers and acquisitions.

Most-Favoured Nations arrangements, or anything similar, can only work effectively if the products and services they cover are a commodity – like paper clips. Even in this situation, a supplier should carefully consider agreeing to terms such as these. They take no account of wider value in a relationship or the circumstances of an individual situation over time.

TIPS & NOTES

One way of countering this is by offering an MFN around what you are prepared to provide, but keep it away from price. For example, we will guarantee that the service level you receive from us will be the same as all our customers in these respects: hours of service, personnel, level of experience of personnel, etc.

Simple or complicated pricing?

It is no surprise that mobile-phone companies have traditionally had very complicated contracts. After all, the service they are providing is actually pretty simple and not so different from a landline telephone, water or electricity – utilities that all generally charge a single flat rate. Most of these utility-style products have some kind of infrastructure to keep them going and some kind of equipment at the point of delivery which needs to be paid for. Mobile phones are amazing pieces of technology, which have had billions spent on their research and development, but the industry was born at a time when it could pretty much dictate pricing and mobile phones were expensive things for people to have – until the operating companies worked out how to bundle up the handsets as part of the pricing model.

It can seem like a minefield to navigate through, but having lots of changing options can make a lot of money and help to prevent comparison between suppliers. This in turn slows down the possibility of products or services becoming a commodity with low-margin pricing, despite a market that is fiercely competitive.

Creating a pricing matrix or 'bundles' like a mobile-phone operator may well not be an option, but the lesson is that simplified or individual pricing leads to harder negotiation and downward pressure overall. It's better to include elements that go together to make up a package.

Consideration should be given to splitting a product or service pricing into parts. And when something of tangible value, or that adds to a supplier's costs, is added to a product or service, consideration should be given as to whether it is included free of charge; even if it is ultimately given away as part of a negotiation. Absorbing additional costs is often not necessary, provided their value can be clearly communicated.

PROJECTS & ACTIONS

- Is your pricing too simple?
- Are you absorbing things you could be passing on, even at cost?
- If you added some extra elements, would it give you a better negotiating position?
- Are there some pure margin add-ons that you could include?

When to introduce pricing

Salespeople in particular seem to be cautious about giving out pricing. Of course they are; they want the deal and don't want to scare anyone off. But instead of opting to spend hours/days/weeks/months talking to a prospective customer with an ever-present big 'elephant in the room', it is clearly important to get at least a vague idea of pricing into the conversation early on, after value has been established. If there is a £1 million project at the end of a process, even if a supplier is a small component of it and it is necessary to make that happen to get the supplier's deal over the line, there is no point in the prospective customer thinking it is only £100,000, or that they don't need the other items to make it work.

Smart salespeople establish value first then get the price out early if they can. It doesn't have to be a blunt number slapped on the desk in an aggressive way or brought up in neon lights, but as a prospective customer is engaged and worked with, the broad pricing should be communicated as early as possible. This way salespeople can make sure they are focusing their time and energy on something that the prospective customer can and will be broadly prepared to pay.

If a lot of input is required from a prospective customer to be able to give them the price, that should be explained to them and the kinds of things that affect the pricing clearly communicated. If it is necessary to indicate that a final price cannot be given until all the information has been collected, then it should be done upfront. This can be built into a sales process so that it is a natural point in any deal.

It may save a lot of time and energy to find out who the discount seekers are at the outset, and whether a prospect has a realistic grasp of what they should be paying for what they are asking for. Those who just want rock-bottom pricing, and are blinkered with regard to anything else, don't usually make the best customers in anything more than commodity sales.

7. The Sales Process

Until now this book has largely been about everything outside the sales process, which is all incredibly important. But how does a supplier take a prospective customer through the journey to buy, and make it a positive activity for both buyer and seller? How much selling is involved? And what is management's role?

This chapter focuses on helping the management of a supplier organisation develop a good sales process – this is often monitored through what is called a 'sales funnel' or 'sales pipeline' – and deals with the basics and how it is developed into a sophisticated device with some simple tools for reference.

In this chapter we will discuss:
- The basis of a good sales process.
- Questions to ask and why.
- A sample sales process.
- Where management should focus their time in the sales process.

- What happens if the prospective customer won't go through the process?
- The role of a proposal in the sales process.
- Customer relationship management (CRM) systems.

The basis of a good sales process

In the Information Age, a supplier's sales process is more important as a focus for management and salespeople. It is the focal point that is used to bring a sale to a successful conclusion, begin the client relationship and bring revenue to a business. Or to discover there is no basis on which to do business. It is where the skill of selling occurs. It is also the process that binds sales functions with other functions of a supplier organisation.

It doesn't have to be complicated, just clearly communicated to all, and something that has value for the prospective customer as well as for the supplier.

It seems commonplace to encounter supplier organisations who either don't have a sales process or have something that is not well implemented or communicated. Sometimes the process seems to be focused purely on the sales function. It also appears commonplace for advice to be given that says, 'Make selling a process', but there is very little advice on *how* to do this.

The sales process is an essential tool for measuring a sales function, what the salespeople are delivering, what is stuck and where, and which projects the business may have to deliver in the future so that management can forecast and plan for them.

There is no reason why each sales process can't be unique to each company or product/service line, because it has to take into account the fundamental requirements of each company to bring a customer on board successfully. One size *doesn't* fit all: and the sales process should not be dictated by a customer relationship management (CRM) system or something similar.

Likewise, there is no suggestion that it is a formula or some kind of rigid set of steps. That would usually result in highly unsuccessful sales practice. It is a framework for tracking activity in the sale so it can add the maximum amount of value where possible and establish meaningful commercial relationships.

On 1 May 1988, Neil Rackham, the then CEO of Huthwaite International, published his book *SPIN Selling*. Obviously, this is now a little dated but, after twenty-five years of being involved in sales, the author still believes that there is no better authority or articulation of the fundamentals of the modern sales process, for two reasons:

1. It is based on millions of dollars of actual research – over 35,000 sales calls.

2. It deals with *larger*, more complex sales. The sales that this book contends with are more common in the Information Age and need skilled salespeople. Sales that require more than one sales call (an interaction with a buyer) to close.

Obviously, thirty years on, with the existence of the Internet, a lot has changed, but with some updating and interpretation for the Information Age, much of the approach still holds true for a sales process, as follows:

In his book, Rackham sets out the principles and basics of a sales call which should be incorporated into any sales process (Rackham's chapter titles in brackets):

Introduction ('Preliminaries')
Set the environment and create a space to exchange honest information.

- Does this company match the ideal customer profile developed in Chapter 5? If so, by how much?
- Can a confidential relationship be established in which there is an exchange of honest information?
- Is the salesperson able to ask the questions necessary to uncover the customer's needs?
- On the surface, is there an opportunity to do business that should be explored further?

Uncovering motive ('Investigating')
Asking questions and investigating is the most important sales skill for salespeople involved in larger sales. (See below for 'Questions Ask and Why'.) Asking questions uncovers the customer's problems and develops their needs. As Rackham observed, there are two types of needs:

- *'Implied Needs'.* These are the starting point in larger sales. They are the problems, difficulties or dissatisfactions of a prospective client. Uncovering these can be enough for someone to buy in a smaller sale (one that involves a short engagement with the customer by the salesperson).

- *'Explicit Needs'.* These are the strong wants and desires of a customer. These are key in successful larger sales and business-to-business sales in the Information Age. Successful salespeople treat *Explicit Needs* differently from *Implied Needs.* They will use questioning (see below) to convert *Implied Needs* into *Explicit Needs* in order to find the solution for the customer.

Is there a fit? ('Demonstrating Capability')

This is the critical stage of a prospective supplier demonstrating their ability to solve the prospective customer's problems – their *Explicit Needs.*

- This will be through clear and concise demonstrations of products, services, value provided by the supplier, business models and so on.
- These demonstrations of capability will focus on the direct *benefits* that fill the customer's *Explicit Needs* which have been uncovered as part of the process.

Conclusion/decision ('Obtaining Commitment')

- Every sales process should be built from a series of commitments ('Advances') from a prospective customer, eventually ending in a decision to go with the supplier or not or to 'close' the deal.
- As Rackham discovered, in larger sales regularly taught 'closing techniques' are ineffective and are likely to harm the chances of actually closing a sale. (See

salestribe.blog/closing-techniques for a discussion on traditional closing techniques.)

- Completing a deal should always be looked at as the beginning of a relationship. 'Closing' is not a good term for completing deals in the Information Age.
- In bigger sales, which mean bigger decisions, the more pressure a customer is put under to finish a deal the less likely they are to make a positive decision to move to order or sign.

The principles don't need to be much more than the above on a basic level. Obviously, in practice, they might take more to execute it, or they can be very simple. The detail specific to an individual business is very important.

TIPS & NOTES

» Successful salespeople spend most of their time on the Uncovering motives and Is there a fit? stages.

» Successful salespeople will summarise the benefits after a potentially long meeting or session to key points.

» There is nowhere in the basics of the sales process where the salesperson or anyone in the organisation is pushing anything on anyone. There is no convincing, persuading or defending what has been proposed, nor the features or benefits of a particular product or service – all things associated with 'traditional' sales.

» It is important that resources from the supplier organisation may need to be made available to the salesperson to assist them in executing the tasks identified in the sales process. These should be clearly defined in the process and expected to be used in this way by the relevant individuals and teams in the supplier's organisation.

» The prospective customer may need to make its own

---

resources available. If it can't or won't, it is usually unlikely that the sales process will succeed and it should be established early on in the sales process whether this is a likely obstacle.

» The conversations through the sales process will explore all elements in order to find a way for the businesses to engage. At the end of the process, the two organisations will decide on whether it is right to move ahead or not. Usually the customer is in control of whether a deal will move ahead or not but, as discussed in Chapter 1, Attitude and Approach, the supplier can also choose to say no.

» The sales process should (usually) present what is known as a 'two-way street': a reciprocal set of actions for two parties to see if there is a fit to do business.

» The job of the salesperson is to set the scene and establish the environment in which conversations can be had; questions should be asked to uncover needs and problems, and then to see if there is a way to solve them by demonstrating capability and identifying value.

» Pricing will normally only be introduced once the salesperson has established the value their organisation brings as part of filling the *Explicit Needs* (strong desires) of a customer. A customer is much more likely to move forward with a purchase if these needs are built up to hold a value far greater than the cost of the product or service.

» To measure success in the stages of moving through a sales process, the salesperson must obtain commitment from the buyer. Getting a comment such as 'good presentation' is not a commitment, nor is an 'I will drop you a line sometime to come and present the product again'.

» Commitment is a specific action to advance the sale – and a good sales process documents that commitment. In simple selling a commitment is getting an order but in complex sales it is a tangible step towards establishing a relationship to do business. For example, 'I would like you to come back next week and present to the other members

continued

of the team and the boss.' Or 'We would like to trial the service for x time.' Management should ensure the questions asked by a salesperson in the process should be designed to obtain this commitment. Salespeople should propose the commitment they are looking for – but it should be realistic about where the parties are in the relationship.

Questions to ask and why

Questions are one of the most important aspects of selling. Planning and preparing for the questions that will be asked to uncover the needs and problems of a prospective customer is crucial. These are all questions asked to uncover motive – in the *'Investigating'* stage. As Rackham found in his research into his book *SPIN Selling*, the right questions have a strong relationship to sales success. But what kind of questions?

• *'Closed Questions'* or *'Open Questions.'* For many years traditional selling courses and manuals have talked about the differences between these two types of questioning and their role in the sales process. A *closed question* is one with a 'yes' or 'no' answer, whereas an *open question* elicits a longer answer from the customer – the idea is that the prospective customer will talk more with *open questions* thereby revealing more information which can then be used to help the sale. Rackham found no evidence in his research that successful salespeople in larger sales asked more or fewer *open* or *closed* questions – and, even more surprisingly, that anyone had ever done any credible research to validate such practice.

Rackham uncovered his own set of questions, or 'SPIN' sequence, which were shown to be asked by many successful salespeople and to have a positive influence on the sales process. A supplier who is researching ideal customers, as in Chapter 5, is unlikely to need the first two types of questions for anything more that validation:

- *'Situation Questions'*. These are the questions that successful salespeople used at the beginning of a sales call to establish the facts and background situation of a prospective customer. If overused they can irritate a buyer, so successful salespeople use them sparingly. With the availability of research tools in the Information Age, it is often not necessary to ask the customer these questions directly, but to validate the research which has been done prior to engagement. They should be used only enough to confirm a fit to an ideal customer profile (Chapter 5). Examples of these type of questions could be: 'How many people work for your company?' or 'What are your company's revenue targets for the next year?'
- *'Problem Questions'.* After enough *situation questions* have been asked, successful people move on to questions that uncover problems – more likely to fit with the psychographic and behavioural aspects of an ideal customer. 'How could the support you receive from your current supplier be improved?' or 'What quality issues do

you have around your current output with that product?;
or 'Doesn't the training level of the operators required
to use that machine mean it is difficult to use?' Again, a
lot of these questions may be easy to answer through
research upfront and only be validated as assumptions in
communication with the customer.

• *'Implication Questions'.* Rackham found that smaller sales
could be executed very effectively by asking good *situation*
and *problem questions*, and then by introducing benefits
to the prospective customer. This is most likely why, in
the Information Age, smaller sales, which require less
interaction with salespeople, will largely be able to be
completed without them.

Successful larger sales, however, required salespeople to ask
a much more complicated and sophisticated question which
relied on their domain knowledge of the product or service
sector. He called this the *implication question. Implication
questions* uncover the seriousness of a problem and create
some urgency around the need to solve that problem. They
convert *implied needs* to *explicit needs* by increasing the scale
of the problem so that the customer realises that what they may
perceive to be an unimportant issue is actually much bigger.

Examples of these are: 'Doesn't this problem mean you
are unlikely to hit your targets this year?' or 'How many
support calls do you receive because of this issue? What
level of service staff do you have to employ to deal with
the customer fallout?' Rackham found that these are
especially powerful with decision makers – he calls them
'the language of decision makers'.

- *Need-payoff questions.* These are questions that cement the value of a product or service in a prospective customer's mind. They should be asked after *implication questions.* They get *the customer to tell the salesperson* the benefits that a product or service has to offer. 'If we were able to help you raise your revenues by 20 per cent, how would that affect you?' or 'If your offering attracted 50 per cent more unique users, what would happen to your sales?' and 'If your production process was twice as fast but half as complicated, what would that mean for your output?' These are all *need-payoff questions* that successful salespeople ask. They shouldn't be too simple or risk patronising the buyer. They should never be asked when the salesperson doesn't have the answers to those questions.

Asking good *need-payoff questions* generally requires the salesperson to be experienced in their market so that they are then able to work with the customer to provide the answers. And it typically involves the salesperson being able to build a numbers-based business case and have a clear understanding of it.

Need-payoff questions shouldn't be asked too early in the engagement with the customer. They should only be asked when the salesperson has developed the needs of the customer, which often means that quite a good relationship has been established with a decent level of credibility.

TIPS & NOTES

» A good salesperson will look carefully at the set of questions that they need to use in their engagement with the prospective customer in advance. These will be modified and updated for each encounter.

» A good salesperson will establish who they are, why they are talking to the customer (but without giving in-depth product or service details) and a right to ask questions by establishing credibility. They will establish clear roles – as the seller, they are a seeker of information; the buyer should be the giver. A salesperson who is answering all questions in an engagement with a prospective customer hasn't sufficiently established their role as a questioner.

» Listening carefully to the answers and recording them in notes is obviously essential in any complex sales environment.

» There needs to be some validation that the information is true about a prospect, or the situation they are in. If assumptions are made that are important for the deal to work, the salesperson needs to be unafraid to ask those questions as part of the process. The Internet can be a wildly inaccurate source of information so everything from there should be validated carefully with the prospective customer.

» If there is an assumption, for example, that a product or service will be placed in a specific location on a website or used or marketed by the prospective customer in a certain way, as part of their offering, then it should be clarified that this is definitely the case, and meaningful commitments should be attached to this as part of any deal.

» It is unlikely that any service or product will fully fit the customer. Where possible, a good salesperson will ask questions that build the value and establish benefits that far exceed the negatives that are introduced through these mismatches. Of course, there are always cases that are a complete mismatch and this will typically mean there is no point continuing in the process. But the reverse is also true – there may be no match on the surface but the salesperson can unlock a clear opportunity once they have learned about the customer's business.

» Often prospective customers will think they know all that they need to fix a problem. Customers react more positively when they are treated as experts. The salesperson should be leading them to find their own problems through the questions they ask. This should be backed up with stories and case studies of where things have been successful and, wherever possible, using statistics to build value and credibility and demonstrate capability.

» A smart salesperson will often need to use the answers to questions to build a numbers-based business case to make sure the deal works for both parties – this is a part of working out if there is a fit. It is often a sensitive area to start asking questions around numbers of their business so this is often where tact and empathy come into play, along with confidentiality, in order to glean the correct information necessary. If there are holes in the numbers, it should be a showstopper.

» In larger sales, features and advantages will rarely be the things that drive a successful sale. In smaller sales, they are far more likely to be significant – 'The X450 has twice as many speed settings as the X350', for example.

Objections

Traditional selling techniques have explored how a salesperson should overcome objections. Again, referencing Neil Rackham's extensive research in *SPIN Selling* is validated by the author's experience over many years.

As discussed in Chapter 1, Attitude and Approach, a salesperson needs a level of intelligent persistence and to be able to handle sometimes initially difficult or aggressive customers.

But the following considerations should be made with regard to objections in the sales process:

- There will always be objections between a seller and a buyer. In some cases, these will prevent a deal being done.
- It is critical that new objections aren't *introduced* by the salesperson. One way of introducing them is by talking about the benefits and advantages of a product or service before uncovering the true needs of the customer.
- Objections, particularly on price, occur when the salesperson hasn't developed the needs of the customer to be sufficiently strong enough. If a salesperson is just talking about features and advantages, it is likely that they will receive lots of objections. Instead, they should focus on asking *problem*, *implication* and *need-payoff questions*; and introducing a solution through those.

PROJECTS & ACTIONS

- Consider the sales process and how it operates in your business. How does your organisation continually obtain commitment from the prospective customer through the steps of the sale? Use the information in this section to develop a process that will work for your organisation; a process that the relevant people in the organisation can follow, and which can be adapted to your company as it changes over time. (There is a sample sales process below.)
- Make sure your organisation approaches sales calls with the right questions. These should be worked up in advance of any meetings with prospective customers – using role play here really helps in a group or one-to-one:
  a. Your *situation questions* should be developed as part of the ideal customer profile (Chapter 5).

---

b. Write down a few potential problems the buyer might have that can be solved by your product or service.

c. Write down the *problem questions* that may be asked to uncover those.

d. *Implication questions* should be practised and prepared in advance. For each problem anticipated, salespeople should write down four implications a problem might throw up that may make it more severe than it might have seemed. Questions should then be developed from those implications to lead the buyer to the problem.

e. *Need-payoff questions.* These questions encourage the buyer to tell you the benefits of your product or service in their own words. Only to be used after developing the needs and if you have the answers. Use the *implication questions* you asked to trigger the *need-payoff questions.* Care should be taken not to make these too simple or patronising – such as *'Would you like to save money?'*

A SAMPLE SALES PROCESS

Here is a sample sales process – this can be called a 'sales funnel' or 'sales pipeline'. Each stage of the process needs a clear commitment from the prospective customer to move forward. A salesperson should always be looking for that commitment so as to demonstrate progress.

The basic sales process example

Suspect - Opportunity / Fallback
- Potential future opportunity
- No next steps
- No appointment
- Possible suspect

↓   ↑

Made Contact / First Discussions
- Convert 'Suspect' to 'Prospect'
- Commitment obtained to move forward
- Basic set of questions asked/answered
- Scheduled meeting obtained

↓   ↑

Customer Needs Discovered / 25%
- Deeper questions asked/answered
- Obtained commitment for demonstration
- Commitment to supply data for defining economics
- Commitment for any resources for sales process
- Next step scheduled

↓   ↑

Commited Prospect / 50%
- Solution/proposal presented
- Key decision makers on-board
- Defined economics
- Any implementation timeline / project length discussed
- Commitment to work towards broad deal terms

↓   ↑

Likely Customer / 90%
- Broad deal terms agreed/signed
- Contracts/terms of business submitted for review
- Any negotiation taking place
- Commitment on clearly defined project

↓   ↑

Relationship established
- Deal signed
- Active customer
- Say 'thank you'
- Invoice
- Ask for referral

Opportunities/fallbacks

- *Each salesperson has a list of potential opportunities generated through the lead generation techniques discussed in Chapter 8, Engage. Usually, this should be contained in a customer relationship management (CRM) system (discussed below).*
- *This list contains the names of companies that either haven't been contacted yet, or they have been but may not fit right now. They will be categorised as suspects, as discussed in Chapter 5, An Ideal Customer Profile.*
- *Each suspect organisation can be here multiple times with different opportunities.*
- *It is crucial that good notes about any contact and all research are taken in a notes repository such as a CRM system throughout the process.*

Made contact

- *Customers listed at this stage have been contacted, either by phone or in a face-to-face meeting (or several).*
- *Research has been done on the individuals involved, their roles and the people around them who need to be involved by the salesperson. The salesperson may even suggest to the buyer the people they may normally need to involve in the process to conclude a deal.*
- *Customers at this stage have answered or validated a set of basic questions about their business, as*

145

developed in Chapter 5, An Ideal Customer Profile. They will begin to be considered prospects – customers who may fit the ideal customer profile.

- *The salesperson will have presented basic company information; if possible, the salesperson will introduce stories about success to establish credibility and to introduce the company as experts (see Chapter 4, Becoming an Expert).*

- *To move forward, the salesperson will need to obtain commitment from the prospect to explore the opportunity further. This might be a further meeting with the right people with a clear agenda to explore needs.*

TIPS & NOTES

» The salesperson will have explained the sales process which will be necessary to follow to move forward, including what resources may be required from both sides.

» There may have been several attempts to get to this stage.

» This may take several encounters over a period.

» No features or advantages will be introduced at this stage.

» It is not good to bad-mouth competitor suppliers. Good salespeople talk about the value they add and provide examples of where they have excelled in cases where they know the customer may be experiencing professional pain without referring to the competitor organisation causing the problem.

» Is there any legal documentation that needs to be completed, such as the signing of a non-disclosure agreement (NDA)? This may also be added as an indication of commitment.

Customer needs discovered

- *This is where the 'Questions to Ask and Why' section (above) should be used to uncover needs.*
- *Prospects at this stage will have answered enough questions to have uncovered needs or problems to ensure that the product or service a supplier is offering fits.*
- *The salesperson will normally have obtained commitment for a demonstration of the product or service.*
- *The salesperson may have obtained commitment for the customer to supply data for defining the economics of doing business.*
- *The buyer and seller have agreed to commit resources to the sales process to explore it further.*

TIPS & NOTES

» It is important that all notes and data are verified with the prospect so that they are accurate.

» Any assumptions that have been made need to be worked through to be turned into accurate facts about the customer's situation.

Committed prospect

- *At this stage the prospect will have been presented with solutions to the identified needs and problems.*
- *There should be defined economics (pricing, payment terms, costs of delivery, cost of ownership, etc.) around the solution which have been shared, discussed and agreed by the customer.*

- *A proposal may have been presented (see below).*
- *Key decision makers should be on board. Who the key people are who need to sign off a deal. Most importantly, all who can say no.*
- *There should be an implementation and decision time frame discussed and agreed by all stakeholders in both organisations.*
- *The prospect should give commitment to sign some sort of 'Heads of Terms', or purchase order, or have provided clear acknowledgement that the terms of business are acceptable so as to move to the next stage.*
- *'Go or no-go decision' should be taken by the supplier organisation involving relevant stakeholders.*

TIPS & NOTES

» Really good notes along with a business case should be captured on the process and the deal at this stage so it can be reviewed by others in the supplier organisation.

» Any risks or assumptions that still need to be clarified should be clearly identified where applicable. Small details can often be critical to advancement.

Likely customer

- *There is a defined project and agreement that has been approved by both parties in clear documentation.*
- *Contracts/terms of business are submitted for review.*
- *Negotiating is taking place on business terms.*

- *The salesperson needs to get commitment from the customer to sign the agreement to do business or to place the order.*

Relationship established

- *Congratulations! Salesperson/management says 'thank you' to the customer. (There is no substitute for a handwritten card, note or similar here.)*
- *Ask for a referral?*
- *Invoice.*

The following two additional steps are often overlooked but are usually an important part of finishing the process, depending on the supplier organisation.

Implementation, launch and handover

- *Often salespeople are not required to continue with a project once the deal has been signed. But usually in this case there should be an organised handover process to relevant staff.*

Monitor, upsell and continuation

- *As discussed in Chapter 2 (Basic Types of Sales Roles) and in Chapter 11 (Looking After Existing Customers), which deals with maximising the relationship with customers and who should be responsible.*

Where management should focus their time in the sales process

Management's function in the sales process should be on the following key areas (after establishing the sales process):

- Regularly monitor the metrics that are established (see Chapter 10).
- Explore how to evolve the conversion rates for each stage *and* for the overall process, i.e. how to make the process more efficient.
- Rigorous checking that, as each deal moves through the stages, they have really fulfilled the criteria and obtained the commitment necessary to move to the next stage.
- Attention should be given to supporting salespeople in negotiation and finishing the deals.

TIPS & NOTES

There should be some calculation of 'conversion'. Conversion is the number of prospective customers that need to be added to the beginning of the sales process to yield a customer at the end of it. Once a sales process is established, this should be a key measurement. Obviously this also helps a company measure the quality of the leads it is generating over time.

What happens if the prospective customer won't go through the process?

It is important for a supplier to establish very early on that the value of the sales process is there for both the selling organisation and the customer. If someone won't follow it, it is unlikely that a deal will be able to be concluded.

It doesn't need to be an arrogant statement; just presenting the facts beforehand is enough. If the prospective customer wants to jump straight to price and the supplier has a fixed price, it may be possible to disclose it. But for many businesses today, it isn't as simple as just a price, as we have discussed in this chapter and in Chapter 6 – pricing alone will probably not cover the full value of dealing with the supplier organisation. Good salespeople generally don't talk price until they have established value with the customer.

Deals done outside a process can result in the worst relationships and the worst customers.

If the supplier decides to say 'no', it should have clear reasons why that is the case and should try hard to keep the door open for a prospective customer if/when they want to re-engage.

Sometimes there is simply a personality clash between the salesperson and the prospective customer, which is worth monitoring.

The role of a proposal in the sales process

Sales proposals should serve the following roles:
- As a container of information derived from the process – which nowadays can be so much more than a document

- clearly and systematically laying out the conversations between the supplier organisation and the prospect organisation.
• To support the person or team the salesperson is working with in the prospect's organisation.
• To present the needs and problems of a prospect, and the solutions to those needs.
• To represent discussed and agreed business terms.

A proposal is neither a place to make undiscussed assumptions by the supplier or the prospective customer, nor the time to introduce commercial aspects of the deal that have not been discussed previously in the hope that no one will notice.

The proposal can be an amazing thing, but, all too often, it is a long, dry template document that has lots of outdated information that is not read and a space at the back where the commercial terms are first introduced. As a result, the prospect doesn't read any of it apart from the pricing in the last page or two.

If the salesperson has done their job properly, and a proposal is still needed, it should not contain anything that hasn't been discussed before – including pricing – unless specifically requested by the customer.

The best proposals are often not long documents. Busy people prefer good-looking, easy-to-read documents that are succinct and present the relevant details in a digestible format. Consideration should be given to whether the only thing that needs to be presented to the customer is simply a set of terms. Certainly after many rounds of negotiation, it is not a given that the prospect will want to have to wade through pages and pages of information before getting to what they are interested in. It is a good idea to talk to them and ask them what is required.

HOLDING OUT FOR THE PROCESS

When we were building a technology business, our business model was to license a piece of software to a customer and then share in the revenues that software generated when it was used by the customer's end-consumers. As a result, it was essential that we established an environment in which the prospect could share confidential information so they could give some idea what they might earn from the software, so that we, in turn, could price based on the size of their business, so as to be fair to our other customers.

There was one mid-size customer, definitely worth having and a household name. The person responsible in that company for our part of the business was a senior manager reporting to the founder/owner and other senior executives, so he was in possession of the information that we needed.

We established a fantastic relationship and enjoyed many great meetings with the prospect. For three years, we met every few months at their office, at our office and at trade shows. But he would never share the information we needed and each time our meetings ended with a frustrating impasse. Until, eventually, the customer realised that he really wanted our products, but that he wouldn't get them unless we went through this process together.

He shared enough to give us what we needed, we gave him a fair price and, after a bit of negotiation, we cut the deal.

He became a good customer, friend and long-term ally of our company, referring us to many other contacts along the way as people he respected.

Customer relationship management (CRM) systems

In the Information Age it is impossible to write a book on sales without talking about some of the tools that a company should consider using. A customer relationship management (CRM) system can be considered a strategic asset to a business if it is chosen carefully and implemented and used correctly.

The CRM system should ultimately contain every potential company a supplier can sell to, the contact details of relevant people, the communications that have been had with them and where they are in the supplier's sales process. The knowledge shouldn't be in the salesperson's head and they can't take it with them if they leave. It should be considered a corporate asset and every bit of work salespeople do increases the value of the asset.

There are interesting breakthroughs in the realms of 'big data' and artificial intelligence (AI) which can increasingly automate the collection of contact information, preferences of prospects and their output on social media. As these tools evolve and link data and social networks with customer information, they will add significant value, but only if they are used intelligently.

An essential component of any CRM system today is for it to support 'inbound' marketing – this is the linking of the system to social media, websites, blogs and so on, so that it can track the activity of prospective customers and feed the salesperson with the information so they can act on it when contact with the customer is made. (See 'Inbound Marketing' in Chapter 8, Lead Generation.)

A CRM system should not dictate the sales process of a supplier organisation. It should be able to adapt to the specific process a supplier needs to go through, as developed as a result of this chapter.

An entire book could be written on CRM systems, and this is an ever-changing area which is being disrupted massively by new technology, businesses and business models. A blog post on CRM systems is available at www.salestribe.blog/crm-systems

8. Engage

Following the chapters and exercises in this book should mean that individuals and organisations now have the right attitude, know their product or service and are armed with material. In addition, the company and team have a plan for establishing themselves as experts in the market(s). They know what an ideal customer might look like to them, what questions they are going to ask, and management have a valuable sales process that they and the customer should go through to bring deals to the company.

In this chapter we will discuss:
- Elevator pitches.
- Start selling when there is no active process.
- Lead generation.
- Targeting.
- Dealing with retail companies and procurement departments.

Elevator pitches

In the Information Age the amount of information that people are dealing with daily is vast. It means attention spans are increasingly challenged. Most organisations continue to target with a sort of 'spray' of information: a detailed and complicated pitch, which involves presentations, documents, websites and other long-form marketing materials. As most of it isn't looked at or read, the message is often lost in the process.

Most people are busy and don't want to listen to lots of pitches. Even the people whose job it is to get pitched to don't receive pitches from new people all day long. Many people are pitched to repeatedly and aggressively, without any regard for them as a person. It is a sure way to push them back into their comfort zone with their existing supplier relationships.

Of course, a supplier organisation needs to pitch to start the conversation. Coupled with the attitudes and approaches discussed in Chapter 1, an organisation should have a nice punchy and succinct elevator pitch, which is the enabler for a deeper conversation.

Once this has been developed, everyone necessary in a company can use it as the basis for their outbound communication. It can be adapted as required and people don't have to stay 100 per cent 'on message', or word for word; but, done well, it will give them the ingredients with which to stimulate interest – and most importantly, a further conversation. It can also be used to start establishing the salesperson as a questioner.

An elevator pitch also helps with confidence since the individuals know pretty much exactly what to say when they communicate with someone. But, as we discussed in Chapter 7, The Sales Process, they aren't going to try and introduce their company and every feature of a product or service in seconds.

An elevator pitch assumes that the person pitching has just walked into an elevator with someone. They have the time from the moment the lift doors close to when they open – say, between twenty and thirty seconds – to introduce themselves to that person. Here are some of the considerations when developing an elevator pitch:

- It should be kept simple and punchy.
- It introduces the person first, and what they do.
- It is a good place to start presenting the organisation or individuals as experts: 'We are experts in x, y, z.'
- It should introduce why the approach followed is different, or makes a difference, but stay away from product or service features and benefits.
- It may introduce needs or problems that the organisation can fix.
- It may be an introduction to a story which stimulates two-way dialogue.
- In approach it should be delivered with confidence and enthusiasm, but not be too keen and pushy. It should be friendly and delivered with a smile.

MY ELEVATOR PITCH

'Hi, I'm Steve. I've been working in sales and commercial teams for twenty-five years and I'm the CEO of Sales Tribe Limited. We are a company that focuses on helping organisations structure and run highly successful salespeople in the Information Age. We do this by identifying problems that are likely to get worse and offering solutions to fix them.'

'What kinds of problems?'

'The Information Age is pushing the boundaries covered by traditional sales techniques, deals are generally larger and more complex. Smaller deals are able to be done without the intervention of a salesperson. It is becoming difficult, if not impossible, to find good salespeople. This is mainly because the organisations they work for are unable to provide a suitable environment and structure to foster an exceptional commercial approach. I have some resources that explore this. Would you be interested in taking a look?'

Or

'How are you fixing them?'

'I have a book and a bunch of other resources which help with organisational structure, plus a support network in the form of a community. I just wrote a paper on great elevator pitches. Would you like a copy?'

From then on, if possible, questions should be asked about their business, or their role in that business, to start building a picture and uncover needs – the questions developed in Chapter 5, An Ideal Customer Profile, and Chapter 7, The Sales Process.

This is not a 'hard sell' and a conversation can be as short or as long as it needs to be to break the ice. It also works across nearly all communication mechanisms, from phone, email and face-to-face meeting to social media.

If it feels pushy or they clam up, then perhaps the product/service isn't for them. It is possible to not know why; it may just not be the right time; they may not like the salesperson's shoes, or their nose! The priority should be to get contact details, as well as their permission to add them to a contact list, so may lead to something one day.

Practise, practise, practise

Great engagement comes from practising it. There is no substitute for it. It should be a routine that is practised every day, if possible.

PROJECTS & ACTIONS

- Create an elevator pitch which is punchy, concise and relevant. Involve other parts of the company with the salespeople and make it a fun activity! It should be the basis from which you can all engage.
- Set a regular date to review the pitch and adapt it as necessary.

Start selling when there is no active process

> **TIPS & NOTES**
>
> A good salesperson should recognise that just because someone isn't coming to them and telling them they are looking for something, it doesn't mean they shouldn't be working the ground. Just because a potential buyer isn't ready to buy now doesn't mean they won't be one day.

Management should ensure that the sales approach is to be well networked even if there is no immediate opportunity. No opportunity should be written off just because it isn't instantaneous. Things change in target organisations. Even the biggest, most arrogant organisations have change forced upon them – now more than ever before. Being persistent without being pushy should be the approach – reminding the buyers that there is always a conversation that can be had when the time is right. Organisations with people in them who may be considered never to yield an opportunity will suddenly do so without having to do anything more than the supplier being on the prospective customer's radar.

Selling is often a process of communicating with people regularly until an opportunity is uncovered that is a win for both parties. It is not right to expect only to pitch when there is a clear and well-defined opportunity.

It is highly likely that rivals will be having these conversations if the salesperson is not.

Lead generation

Lead generation seems to be what instils the most fear in the salesperson. But it shouldn't be too much of a problem to come up with a list of companies to target as a business, in any specific market. And it is getting easier. Now, often, the problem is quality, not quantity.

If the company is not selling into a naturally specific market, it should identify one, two or three market segments and focus on them. It is normally clear who the market leaders are in a sector. Generalists are going to be the first people affected in the Information Age, since non-industry-specific selling will be largely automated in the near future, in the same way that mainstream consumer selling will be.

In any given market, there is no substitute for doing the research and identifying the targets to put into the beginnings of the sales process. Leads need to be found somewhere.

TIPS & NOTES

You will often hear people say, 'I don't have the contacts' — it is much easier than you think to find them with a little persistence!

Finding people to engage with

An existing network
It would be highly unusual to start a business with no network in a market at all. It should be safe to assume that even at the start-up or a small-business level, the business has

been founded to solve a problem or need, and that at least the founders, board and the employees know who the main protagonists are that they want to target.

PROJECTS & ACTIONS
FIND PEOPLE IN EXISTING NETWORKS

There is a fairly simple exercise to start a targeting process using your own networks, which can be also achieved by using various software tools – especially a customer relationship management (CRM) system.

- List all the target businesses that you know already by target categories and ask your colleagues to do the same.
- Go through and mark them with 'Have the right contact', 'Have contacts not right' and 'No contact'.
- Add the resulting list to the CRM system (or equivalent) and the salespeople can start to match them to your ideal customer profile discussed in Chapter 5.
- There are a few ways for your salespeople to identify the right buyers in an organisation. Here the Information Age is coming to work for you. Companies spend significant sums putting information right into salespeople's hands.
  a. Read press releases and search to find who the right contacts are.
  b. Use social media tools, such as LinkedIn, to find the relevant individuals.
  c. Use software tools (see www.salestribe.blog/list-generation for a list) to find the right contacts in an organisation along with their contact information. A lot of these tools are tightly integrated with modern CRM systems.

Generating leads outside your network

For a number of organisations, generating new leads sits in the marketing area of responsibility and not sales. Whether this is true or not, the sales function should always be intrinsically linked to the process of lead generation. There should be a tangible (measurable) return on investment (ROI) case for each activity. Activities where there is no tangible ROI should be limited and minimised. Smart companies use tools to measure all activities to monitor what is successful.

Having the right subscriptions and tools
In the Information Age it is very important that a supplier has the latest, most up-to-date subscriptions and tools that they use for lead generation. There is constant innovation in this area. Tools such as the CRM system and the subscriptions that are tightly coupled with it can provide a significant edge. A list of targeting tools can be found at www.salestribe.blog/list-generation

---

TIPS & NOTES

No list, lead, publishing company and so on will take away the need for your salespeople to do the hard work of matching your company to a target company once the lead has been generated. These sources can provide you with data, but your sales team must take it from there.

Here is a set of ten lead generation areas that should be explored for any business:

1. Websites and social media destinations
- A supplier's website is the most likely place a business-to-business (B2B) buyer will start a buying process.
- Modern websites, social media apps and other digital destinations should support the salesperson with the latest tools available. For example, CRM systems, form

management and list generation tools (see www.salestribe. blog/list-generation for website tools).

- 'Inbound Marketing' (see notes below) tools are providing a powerful method of lead generation.
- Opportunity to make contact should be provided through all areas of a website – don't just a rely on a 'contact us' page.

TIPS &NOTES
'Inbound Marketing'

An example of an *inbound marketing* activity would be linking a website to the CRM system so that, when a suspect or prospect browses the website, data are collected about what they have looked at, for how long, etc. When the prospective customer makes contact, the CRM system identifies and matches the browser history with the person and the process of working through whether they are an ideal customer can start. It may trigger an email from a salesperson which says, 'I notice you browsed our pricing page and wondered if I could answer questions about it.'

Inbound marketing can be matched by smart CRM systems with outbound lead generation activity to track prospective customers from a wider scope. This is a much warmer way of generating leads since the prospective customer has shown some interest in your product rather than you actually interrupting someone.

---

2. Software tools that generate lists

- Some (online) software tools now claim to help build lists of customers for suppliers; these are becoming more and more sophisticated as time passes and information becomes better shared. They can no longer be disregarded as a credible source of leads, but should be carefully checked for quality.

- There should always be a strategy for how the data is used. For example, it may be advantageous to use software to find a set of target companies, through the criteria developed from the ideal customer profile discussed in Chapter 5. Different tools can then be used to find a contact specific to a business relevant to the supplier company.
- By combining tools in a smart way, a modern salesperson can develop a very high-quality target list which is owned by the supplier company and not the original list generator. Care should be taken that this target list stays with the organisation and doesn't move with the salesperson. There is a list of some available tools on the blog at www.salestribe.blog/list-generation

3. Trade press databases

- Most markets have a trade press with subscriptions, emailing lists and publications that contain further lists of companies and various bits of information about markets.
- These are now available, in all sorts of shapes and sizes, costs and levels of participation that can be explored, based on the budget available.
- Signing up to the newsletters, publications and websites these media companies offer, and exploring which one(s) may provide an option for quality data, is one strategy for researching relevant sources.
- A lot of databases may now be redundant when set against the online-based software tools explored above, which will provide up-to-the-second information, so care should be taken when exploring this method of lead generation.

4. *Competition*

- Competition is a useful source of potential lead generation.
- If rivals are working with organisations in the same market and are shouting about their activity, it can make a good fit for information.
- By checking press releases, announcements and social media, it is usually possible to build up a picture of strategy and targets. For example, look at the competition salespeople are connecting with on a site like LinkedIn, in order to see who they may be talking to.
- Find out the consultants and advisers they use and engage with them.

5. *Referrals*

- Referrals from existing customers should be treated like gold dust.
- An organisation should not be afraid to ask its existing customers to recommend it to others.
- Warm leads from referrers with an endorsement hold even more weight.
- If it is permitted under the supplier's engagement rules regarding the customer–supplier relationship, implementing a scheme whereby the buyer or customer organisation is rewarded for referring successful business from a new customer to a supplier is often highly successful. (A lot of companies restrict rewards being made to third parties which might be considered bribes.)
- Second best to a direct referral is often a documented case study of successful customers with similar businesses to

the prospects/suspects an organisation is targeting. If it can be achieved in a cost-effective manner, through a video or audio interview, it can often be much better received than printed material.

- Engaging with someone well connected to act as a referee in exchange for some level of remuneration is also worth considering. Affiliates, consultants and generally well-connected individuals in a particular business sector are worth talking to. Any fee should be performance-based only, if possible, and the quality of the introductions (many people claim they are better connected than they are!) should be monitored. Retainers and other arrangements should be avoided. Any contracts should be kept short and it is important to ensure there are no payments when the referee's network has been exhausted. The Information Economy has many more people working as consultants and advisers in these fields than ever before.

6. Events – exhibitions, conferences, trade fairs and markets

- However many tools and platforms are to be used in selling, the Information Age is unlikely to replace the effect of meeting face to face with customers.
- Events are a great way to meet a lot of people, but focus should be on ideal customers and on quality not quantity (see 'Targeting' on page 175).
- The level of participation should change depending on many factors – the organisation, strategic fit, ideal customers in attendance and so on.

- If it is done well, one event can literally change a supplier company's future.
- Suppliers should consider running their own event where they can present their thought leadership as experts in a market or sector.

7. Buying lists

The concept is amazing: someone brings a supplier organisation a pre-vetted list of people who can instantly be identified as prospective customers. The list has all the customer contact details of buyers who are eagerly waiting for the supplier to get in touch, and all the supplier has to do is follow their sales process to convert the relevant ones into customers. Great care should be taken when using lists like these. Consider:

- The introduction of the General Data Protection Regulation (GDPR) in the European Union will largely mean that buying lists like this is either not possible or should be carefully handled.
- Most of these lists are stale and out of date before they are received.
- Recognising people simply by their job titles can mean so many different things – a role such as 'Head of Marketing' can encompass many different responsibilities.
- The exception, perhaps, is trade show or conference lists, which indicate all the attendees who have given permission to be contacted. Attendance at the event makes it more relevant.
- Buying lists doesn't replace a supplier's research regarding

who a potential customer may be and matching them to the ideal customer profile.

- Generally, there are much better tools for finding interested parties in your products in this age – e.g. 'Inbound Marketing' above.

8. Advertising

- Advertising is another sector which is being disrupted consistently and constantly in the Information Age.
- Attention and retention rates of any traditional advertising, and some relatively new ones, are plummeting.
- All advertising should be carefully monitored for return on investment (ROI). But sometimes it is an important part of a marketing strategy.
- From a purely sales perspective, generating and deploying advertising can be a big distraction and should be left to the people outside sales if possible.
- Care should be taken that there is a definitive 'call to action', and that the activity is tracked to see which one is working, which one sends the most qualified leads, and so on.
- Attempting to send all the respondents to a supplier's website is often the best way to start tracking early, particularly if the correct tools and systems are implemented there.
- 'Above-the-line marketing' means using mainstream media (print, TV, radio, outdoor, Internet banners/buttons, etc.) to promote products and services. This can generally be expensive, especially with large campaigns that

business-to-consumer (B2C) businesses employ to attempt to attract many individual consumers.

- Something as simple as a classified advertisement can be a cost-effective way of generating leads but, in complex sales, focus should be kept on what the supplier is trying to achieve – a meaningful dialogue with a prospective customer.

- Digital, typically Internet-based, methods are generally much more measurable than traditional (print, TV, billboard, etc.) advertising.

- Digital technology can be made much more effective by using methods such as 'split variant testing', where multiple advertisements are created and each one is presented to different segments of a database or group of viewers, which is then monitored to discover which one works best. This is now commonplace, should allow segmentation of databases and is quite accurate in targeting.

TIPS & NOTES

Retargeting

One interesting tool in the digital advertising sector is called 'retargeting'. This is a form of advertising that effectively 'follows' potential buyers around the Internet once they have visited the website of a supplier. It uses cookies that are attached to the viewer's browser when they browse a particular page. When the viewer leaves the website, the cookie continues to provide a retargeting provider with the information that was viewed so that advertising can be served to the viewer from the supplier they visited previously, wherever they are on the Internet. Costs can be kept low with this technology since it is only paid when the viewer of the website clicks on a piece of advertising.

9. Press and public relations

- Most industries have trade press publications and electronic newsletters that can be used to develop business opportunities. Writing articles that generate interest achieves two things:

   1. It can generate leads.

   2. It can help establish the writer, or the writer's organisation, as an expert in a market (Chapter 4).

- Some of the trade press might expect contributors to buy advertising with them or to take part in another activity if they publish articles.

- Others keep the editorial side completely unrelated (or say they do).

- If there is the possibility of using national media, investor relations or the financial press, these are also good forms of exposure that may generate sales leads. A plan should be made for a specific call to action or destination.

- As discussed in Chapter 4, Becoming an Expert, anything that is written or published should have real value to a target audience. Consider the example of a regular monthly column in which an industry professional gives an opinion on various things that are happening in the trade community.

10. Distributors/aggregators

- This is more of a channel to market than a lead generation technique but can be considered as a 'cost of sale'.

- For some industries, the quickest way of reaching a large

number of customers without having a large sales team is still through distribution partners.

- Distributors are usually companies with multiple relationships to supply physical goods, whereas aggregators normally bring together non-physical products such as media, games and other 'content'.

- Both distributors and aggregators will usually already have relationships with the organisations with which a supplier may want to do business and can distribute a company's products alongside other suppliers to customers.

- Distributors and aggregators may also offer the opportunity to participate in particular marketing activities.

- Distributors and aggregators can also be useful for finding many smaller customers through one relationship, which can work well provided it is profitable and doesn't create too much support work.

- Distributors and aggregators will typically take a slice of the margin, which can be quite high. As the world shrinks, this area of business is being heavily disrupted since it is much easier to target customers directly.

- Distributors and aggregators should be nurtured in the same way as any direct customer. It is equally important for a supplier to be seen by them as experts in the market. They should receive exceptional support in all areas. Their staff should be treated with care and, if possible, a plan should be implemented to incentivise them somehow to push a supplier's product line over anyone else's.

PROJECTS & ACTIONS

- Research the tools and subscription services that are right for your company.
- Build a plan around how they will be implemented and by whom within the organisation.
- Set responsibilities for tracking, measuring and monitoring regularly to reprioritise where necessary, along with researching and adding new methods of successful lead generation.

Targeting

Who to target in a business?

Who should salespeople target? The CEO/managing director, 'C-level' (e.g. chief product officer (CPO), chief marketing officer (CMO), director level, the head of a department, the profit and loss owner or a vertical specialist? Finance? Legal? Ultimately, the answer is to make sure they find all the people who might say 'no' to a deal. With the following notes:

- Initially targeting the most senior person is not always the best way to go. Much better to start with the person who is directly related to the supplier's area of business, someone who is using a similar product or service now. This may be someone relatively junior in an organisation. Or the profit and loss owner of a particular business.
- There are normally decision makers, of course, but with more complex sales in the Information Age focus should also be on the people who can influence the decision makers.

- Most sales now involve a lot more people within an organisation. There is typically no way a salesperson can meet and work with everyone.
- Good salespeople will turn those they meet into advocates in the business who will continue to sell for them with their colleagues. They do this by building a picture of their needs, as discussed in Chapter 7 on sales process.
- If there is a specific 'buyer' or 'procurement' role, a good salesperson will quickly work out who else they need to work with in addition to that person in the organisation to ask the right questions.

PROJECTS & ACTIONS
WORK OUT WHO TO TARGET

- Write a list of the most likely job title or job responsibility targets to begin with in your ideal customer.
- Make a list of likely influencers and decision makers you normally encounter in a sale which is updated periodically – add this to your sales process.
- Offer to guide a prospective buyer in large organisations through whom they may need to get on board in their own organisations from previous experience.
- As the salesperson works through the process, they should identify who they will try and turn into internal salespeople and adjust their conversations accordingly. 'Internal' salespeople are those who are 'sold in' to the idea of using a supplier and can help to convince their colleagues.
- Notes should be made throughout the process which identify all the people who can say 'no' – this can include finance, legal, compliance, management, and so on. Even a receptionist may be able to influence a deal.

TIPS & NOTES

Notes, notes, notes!

One of the best sources of information about a customer is normally the customer itself. With all the time and energy that goes into identifying, engaging and working with a prospect, it would be counter-productive not to take notes at all levels of targeting and engagement. Management should ensure this is an essential part of the process. The notes should be confidential and shared where only select people can see them, in line with the latest rules around storing and using personal data.

If you have a CRM system, consider carefully whether you want the often sensitive information stored with the contact information. It is perfectly acceptable to track day-to-day contact and then extract more sensitive data from that to build a better, more strategic profile in a different location, which has limited access.

The notes should contain a complete picture of the customer as the relationship develops. Irrespective of whether this is new business or an existing customer, this is your record of information and the notes should capture every meeting and significant event that happens with the customer.

The notes should be the basis of the engagement with the customer, and proposals should be based on these to ensure an accurate picture is gained.

Remember, just because an individual works at a company it doesn't mean that they know everything that is being published or revealed by the company. In the Information Age, a lot of information about a company may be flowing through public sources which may not have been absorbed by its staff. This, coupled with the anecdotal information received in interactions, can allow someone to put together a very detailed picture which dissects their business. The skill is knowing where to look, making some careful assumptions, which can then be checked with the customer for accuracy and build a picture over time.

Management should ensure information regarding the engagement of the company with buyers is captured and controlled by the company and not the salespeople who work for it.

Networking

'Networking events' can be described as a preconceived way of shoving people into a room to 'pitch' to one another. However, there is no doubt that this is often a really good way of meeting lots of people and should be considered a primary targeting activity. How meaningful they are usually comes down to the quality of the event and the people it attracts.

- Like all targeting, networking is about keeping it simple, getting as many relevant contacts as possible that can then be added to the deal-flow and qualified further to try and match with the ideal customer profile.
- It is unlikely anyone will have a deep enough conversation to be too serious. Approaches should be kept light but have some key messages to get over – that is, the elevator pitch, plus maybe an opinion or two about recent events in an industry, the conference the participants just attended, and so on.
- A salesperson needs to work out as soon as possible whether the person they are speaking to (or the room!) falls into the category of prospective customer discussed in Chapter 5, An Ideal Customer Profile.
- When asking questions salespeople should be polite but humble with regard to things they don't know. They will move on firmly when they have finished the conversation and start a new one.
- It should be as 'low stress' an activity as possible. Expectations should be kept low. Just meeting one

potential person who is worth following up with can be deemed a success.

- There can often be a noisy clique of people who already know one another but that doesn't mean they are discussing business or are target customers – often the opposite. Empty vessels make the most noise!

> **TIPS & NOTES**
> There is a great podcast by Tim Ferriss entitled 'How to Build a World-Class Network in Record Time', which is worth listening to (see www.salestribe.blog/building-a-network).

Email

These days, care should be taken when targeting through email. Many different laws are being introduced to stop email from being completely overrun with sales 'spam'.

While there are many other tools for communication, email remains the most popular business tool. Email is not a platform or technology owned by a company so it is undoubtedly the best way of building an 'opt-in' database of prospective customers and having their direct contact. This removes the risk of the ever-changing algorithms of social media one day rendering a list of followers or prospective customers obsolete.

However, email is generally a terrible way of targeting and 'going in cold' as a stand-alone activity. It should be considered alongside other targeting approaches adopted by a supplier organisation. Today email is generally overused, normally too wordy and has a terrible reputation. This story illustrates why email should be considered carefully (and also applies to other targeting techniques):

IT'S NOT ABOUT YOU

I was a vice-president of a large public company, one of the top 250 public companies trading on the main London Stock Exchange. I received a lot of emails from people who wanted to talk to me about their product or service. In nearly 100 per cent of cases these were misdirected. No doubt my company was a large prize for some people as a customer, but most of the time what I was sent was completely irrelevant. So I started gathering common observations from them:

1. *At least 70 per cent of them were regarding something over which I had no direct control or influence, or about a part of the business that I was not involved in. That is because the emails had been sent either as a result of a piece of email software with a list fed into it, or the person concerned had not done their homework on me, the company I worked for or my job function.*

2. *They had a level of self-importance that could be quite earnest from the person at the other end who believed in their product or service, but ultimately had no empathy and understanding of me and/or my company's business, what professional pains I might have and what I might be trying to achieve. They seemed to actively disregard what might be important to me. They*

were not trying to help me, but, rather, were trying to push something onto me. They had done no homework to suggest why their product or service was applicable to me, even though the company published an 800-page annual report, was regularly in the industry news and generally had well-publicised activity within its business. It made even less sense considering most of our employees were active on social media, as far as I could tell. It isn't difficult to do this research and is getting much easier every day.

3. The sender assumed that I would read and act on the email that was sent. Some were pushy, trying to set up a call or expecting me to read long paragraphs containing buzzwords which I was supposed to be impressed by, enough to make me respond. Some were sarcastic, as if I was somehow being coy about not getting back to them. They gave no thought to the fact that I might be overloaded with my own work. And, even if I knew who the right person was to pitch to, why would I forward such a thing? That would impact directly on my reputation with no tangible gain for me.

4. They were mostly followed by additional aggressive follow-ups with similarly misguided messaging which, for the most part, was from some automated system that just filled up my inbox with dross (if, that is, the spam filter hadn't already filtered it).

The thing is, like all of my colleagues, customers, friends and professional contacts, I did have professional pain which I could have used some help in solving. In my case, I needed new revenue streams – something to do with my title may give that away: 'Vice-President (Sales)'. It isn't as if that wasn't public information, just that the people emailing me hadn't thought about me; they were thinking about themselves.

- Emails such as those in the anecdote are the opposite of selling. They give their company a bad reputation and, while they may have a small 'conversion' rate, these are the (outdated) tools of mass-marketers and not of professional salespeople.

- Email works best when there is a supplier-built opt-in list and it is used to mail out something with authority and credible information; something that backs up the claim that the supplier is an expert and has value in its approach.

- Research should be done on why a person is being approached and what they want to read/watch/listen to. It should be personal, relevant and brief! It should say: 'I deliver true value, I want to talk to you about it and I am not going away.' If a potential buyer is receiving 150+ emails a day, cutting through them is important.

- The ideal customer profile (Chapter 5) and the elevator pitch at the beginning of this chapter can be used as a basis.

- No features or advantages should be used in emails; rather, perhaps an invitation to an event or to watch a video demonstrating expertise.

- Buying a list and mailing out to it blindly without doing background work is not a good approach. Apart from being potentially illegal, it certainly isn't professional and doesn't help establish credibility.

PROJECTS & ACTIONS

- Work out how your company will use email as part of its targeting strategy.
- Craft templates for emails that relate to the sales process created in Chapter 7.
- Use an email tool to capture and use opt-in information and build and maintain a list that can be categorised and segmented for different customers (for some email tools see www.salestribe.blog).
- Use your CRM system to monitor what is being sent and received.

Social media for targeting

Social media is the Internet-based equivalent of networking face to face but, since it connects so many people and provides so much information, it can be used very effectively for targeting.

'Big data', commonly understood to mean the volumes of data captured in recent history regarding user behaviour – to segment information and target it accurately – will change a lot of things. Right now, it is early in this digital revolution, but 'big data' coupled with artificial intelligence (AI), which is also in its relative infancy, will challenge and move the status quo irrevocably in the next few years.

People will see, and will expect to see, a personalised experience across most of what they consume. Most people's initial interface with 'big data' will be through their devices and interactions with social media. Social media companies and providers are the most likely place to develop tools around 'big data' which can aid segmentation and identifying potential customers.

The chief beauty about social media for any sales professional is that people are desperate to talk about themselves and put information and commentary into the public arena.

This is gold dust for accurate targeting and doing some background research. An organisation should make the most of this now, since it is also possible that, as times change, people realise what they are actually giving away, and what those T&Cs (terms and conditions) really mean to their privacy with regard to the information they make public.

PROJECTS & ACTIONS

- This is a perfect activity for a 'pre-sales' person identified in Chapter 2.
- Individuals in a sales team should subscribe to any feed or news posts from the relevant industry. Twitter or similar tools group these feeds into relevant topic areas, but the trade press usually also has relevant newsletters that are delivered through social media channels.
- Focus should be on being active in only a few specific feeds, while digesting many others. Without focus, salespeople can spend their days surfing through low-quality information and not generating anything meaningful. It should be an activity to which a short period of time is allocated as part of a daily routine.

- Each social media app or tool requires a different strategy to be developed, disregarding those services that don't apply. Each should be constantly monitored and measured for effectiveness. Notes should be made, and new methodologies should be explored and shared. Old methodologies should be reviewed and discarded when they become redundant.
- Contribution to social channels can be used to try to push target customers back to avenues such as a website. The contribution content should establish a company as an expert in its field and should contain truly valuable information or informed opinion.
- It is a good idea to divide responsibility for different channels between multiple people if possible.
- LinkedIn is a great tool for business-to-business selling. There is a whole strategy about who to link to, how the network works, and, if a significant number of target customers in a supplier's market are on it, providing a training course to salespeople in its use is worthwhile.
- Social media contacts are generally owned by the individual user — consider how to make the connections and interaction part of a CRM system so that they don't leave with the salespeople if they leave the company.
- Use social media mainly to research people, companies and their job roles, which it is possible to do mostly for free, but consider paying for regular use; this can yield much better results than buying lists, and can also be coupled with those to powerful effect.

Cold-calling by phone

Cold-calling can still be an effective way to get through to people. Some people are amazing at this but there are also those who are petrified by cold-calling in this way.

These days in a business-to-business context, it is becoming increasingly rare to be able to get through to a specific individual in any sizeable company who will be receptive to a completely unsolicited phone call. There are myriad tools that can be used to block these calls.

However, with a little persistence it should still be included as one of the important parts of the mix of contact options.

From a business-to-consumer perspective – for instance, selling people insurance at home – cold-calling is potentially nuisance-calling; it is different in a B2B context. Here, it is normally part of someone's job to listen to new suppliers. Especially if they have something valuable to say!

PROJECTS & ACTIONS

Here are some action items to help structure the sales function for cold-calling:

- If your salespeople aren't currently able to cold-call, then consider help to make sure they can.
- What is required is preparation. The information needed is available – the research can be done, usually with public information. Try this: next time you receive a call from someone trying to sell you something, ask them to tell you about your company and what it does, and what they imagine your role to be. Imagine this is one of your salespeople.
- Expectations for a call should be set low, follow the elevator pitch, offer something valuable like attendance at an event or something else that shows the company is an expert in its market. Keep it short and simple.
- It should be part of a salesperson's daily routine.
- Prospective customers shouldn't be spammed, but there should be persistence until there is a plain 'no', and then it should be put on the back burner for a while before trying again.

- Measure the number of calls and success in a week/month to make sure it is part of a routine.
- Set a number of times before you give up – the average salesperson will give up after two or three calls. So perhaps set a threshold at six or seven?
- One tactic for a sales professional is working out the best times to catch people. Sometimes, for example, it is good to call after a switchboard has closed or opened for the day, when there is more likelihood of getting through to an actual person.
- Some people will never accept a call.

Trade show and conference heaven: tactics for survival

Trade shows and conferences can be major hunting grounds for sales professionals today, but how does a salesperson make the most of events like these?

The most important thing is that the diary is filled with things that might actually make a difference to a supplier's business. Preparatory work is essential as in the rest of the sales job: before the show as many good appointments as possible should be made.

PROJECTS & ACTIONS

Management can help by introducing these actions for trade show success:

- Prospective customers who are attending should be asked if they are in a sales process with a competitor supplier – a meeting at a trade show may be a good place to disrupt this process.
- Have some news to tell people about what the company does (product or service or innovation). Don't overload attendees, just focus on one to three headlines.

continued

- Have a good joke or anecdote and perhaps a little industry gossip. It can't be all earnest and serious. Smile!
- Have some sort of quick qualification questionnaire for the people who have been met, especially if exhibiting. This would start to match them to the ideal customer profile developed in Chapter 5. This is no different from qualifying prospective customers in the normal daily sales process, but try and do it more quickly, without skipping important steps.
- Notes should be made somehow! Especially important if it is busy as details will be forgotten.
- Expectations should be low. In complex selling, finishing a deal on the trade show floor is unusual – but it can be used to start or advance the process and to obtain further commitment. It changes the approach if this is generally understood. Getting a business card and the opportunity for a follow-up is a win!
- There is no point giving out a box of business cards and receiving the same if they don't lead to anything; however, sometimes important influencers can be met without it being immediately obvious.
- Salespeople should use their network to get to the places they need to go. If that is a party invitation or an event where some key targets might be, then it is important to try and be at the event.
- Events like these are exhausting for everyone: remember that, and treat people accordingly. Oversell should be avoided. If they have been on their feet all day in back-to-back meetings, save the sales pitch and just help them to relax. They will come around to the product/service stuff in time.
- Salespeople should be careful with the booze. The last thing your prospects/management/colleagues want is to see someone wasted, so discretion is important. And maybe sleep, too!
- Check out the competition. They have spent good money on showing off to the best of their ability – take advantage of that. Disrupting a competitor's sales process with a prospective customer is a good way to win business.

Entertainment and the power of lunch

More and more restrictions are being placed on entertaining prospective and existing customers these days. But it can be a powerful way of asking the questions that are necessary to start the process and develop a relationship.

PROJECTS & ACTIONS

- There are specific anti-bribery laws and most supplier firms have a policy in place, especially regarding people who are not yet customers.
- A supplier organisation needs to review what it will and won't allow its people to do, and be able to check what level of entertainment prospective customers and existing customers are allowed to receive.
- A simple lunch, dinner or a drink can really help. It doesn't have to be expensive or excessive. But it can change a relationship significantly and expose a human side.

ENTERTAINMENT THAT WORKS

One of the most successful activities we had in one business was simply to have a few seats at a football ground. We would invite our customers to see a match with us and buy them a meal on the way there. It was often a good way of being able to talk to them outside the workplace and learn a lot more about their role and their business.

Get on the list: tenders and RFxs

Tenders/Request for X (RFx), Request for Proposal (RFP), Request for Quotation (RFQ), Request for Information (RFI), European Tenders, etc. are designed specifically for the buying organisation to dictate how a supplier should engage with them. They were originally designed for government organisations; indeed, 'European Tenders' have a strict legal process governed by lawyers all the way through.

There are some companies which only work through a tendering process on very large deals in this way. The suppliers engaged with those companies generally have to employ top-class, highly educated employees to build and submit often extremely complicated bids.

Increasingly, this kind of procurement is used more by firms which are not associated with government or a large corporation. Often consultants are employed to run their buying process. The idea is that they provide a supplier with a template for how to gain information, along with all its competitors, in order that they can compare everyone in an 'apples and apples' way. They can then pick the one that suits them best, normally via a published 'points-scoring' system they adopt around certain elements: service, product, pricing, support and so on.

For a small-to-medium-sized (SME) supplier, they should be considered carefully, as they may allow very little scope for demonstrating value, except through price. Before anyone spends their evenings and weekends pulling these together, it should be decided whether there is really a chance of winning a bid.

There are sometimes ways around these buying processes, but only occasionally, and it is down to the relationship with the individuals.

Once a supplier is on the list or 'approved' in some way they can often enjoy preferential treatment and lucrative relationships.

Dealing with retail companies and procurement departments

These two types of engagement are pretty much the same. They have one major thing in common regarding the average B2B sales organisation. That is, instead of the supplier organisation being able to control the sales process – they do. It is possible that a supplier business relies 100 per cent on one or more of these types of relationship, so there is little possibility of a supplier organisation doing anything other than to follow the process that is laid down by the buyer. This area is and will continue to be significantly disrupted by technology, which will change particularly the retail landscape going forward by automating the process greatly.

Retail

- Retail organisations normally employ buyers whose job it is to specialise in a particular sector. Normally, these individuals have a lot of pressure on them since retailing these days is brutally competitive, and a lot of that competition is passed on to their relationship with a supplier, particularly on to the pricing.
- Usually, the relationship will demand the lowest price a supplier can offer, some sort of guarantee that this is the case (see 'Most-Favoured Nations', Chapter 6, Pricing), or that everyone that has been supplied with the product or service has paid the same price.
- Most retailers now see themselves as an environment

where all their 'space' (physical or digital) is part of a marketing activity and so expect some sort of contribution to that marketing effort (merchandising), especially for anything other than just putting a product on their shelves. And sometimes for that.

- Suppliers need to financially support their products being 'sold through' to end-customers. This can be significant where promotions such as taking 'end-cap' displays at the end of aisles, or other merchandising, is required by the retailer, or is something the supplier wants.

- If a supplier doesn't consider performing these marketing activities, it can find itself in a 'chicken and egg' situation where its product doesn't sell because it can't be found by potential buyers. It may be unlikely that the retailer will take on a product in the first place unless the supplier signs up for this support.

- There are normally specific funds, such as a marketing development fund (MDF), which is usually a percentage of a certain order value held by the supplier and is guaranteed to be made available to the retailer to spend on marketing. This is normally negotiated at contract level when the relationship is started. It typically means that the larger retail customers get more marketing funds from the supplier than the smaller ones. This is effectively a further discount on any pricing agreed.

- Seasonal marketing funds and 'above-the-line' contributions are also common.

- 'Bundling' is a common marketing activity where a supplier's product is bundled with other products, or with a selection of other manufacturers' products and promoted at a special price.

- Retailers typically hate to own stock. If a supplier has a physical product and wants to transfer ownership to them, for them to stock, it will be an issue for them as it is value sitting on their books. So it is important to negotiate who will own the stock at relevant times with the retailer. If there is stock with a retailer which is not selling, the supplier may be asked to pay for it to be returned to them.

- If a supplier has a good relationship and a stream of new products that the retailer also wants to stock, it will be expected to come up with creative ways with their buying team to change or write down the value of existing stock. This is often an area of intense negotiation involving senior management on both sides.

- It is possible to work through specialist distributors in a number of sectors to help access to certain retailers.

PROJECTS & ACTIONS

- Whether this is a primary channel for your business or just a part of it, a sales process should be created explicitly for it (Chapter 7).

- Careful management of these relationships takes special skills. Generally, this is not 'selling' in the normal way. Good account management individuals, who are as skilled in spreadsheets as they are in customer relationships, are required here. Their job is to constantly run the numbers so you understand the margins and any risks that you are taking with products stocked, and how that works. They should also be capable of negotiating a position for you to take with the buyers or distributors.

- Consider exploring creative ways to cope with the issue of stock. Shortening delivery times to reduce the amount of stock purchased by a retailer, or the retailer not taking ownership at all, are possible solutions.

9. Finishing a Deal

Congratulations! A deal has gone through the sales process and there is now a negotiation to finish it with a customer. If the process has been followed, all the relevant questions have been answered, there should be a clear framework to do business, all the people on the customer's side are on board and the commercial terms are clear. But it isn't finished yet! Until the documents are signed the deal is not done and, in many cases in more complex deals, this is where the hard work starts.

This chapter is designed to help management with the contractual approach and how to negotiate the finishing of a deal. In this chapter we will discuss:

- Salespeople's attitude to signing contracts.
- Types of contracts.
- Negotiating commercial contracts.
- Losing a deal.

Salespeople's attitude to signing contracts

Many salespeople talk about the contractual element of doing a deal as if it is a serious pain in the proverbial backside. A blocker between them and the signature of the deal, which of course it is – for a reason! A lot of salespeople don't really have any knowledge of the legal elements and see it as something that should be left to the lawyers. But if salespeople want to finish a deal successfully, then, typically, they will need to have a signed contract. If their commission depends on signing legally binding documentation, which it should, then it makes sense for them to understand what that might look like. It also makes sense for them to understand what they will be asking a customer to sign up to so they are able to introduce it throughout the sales process: 'If we are going to do business, you will need to be able to agree on x, y, z', and so on.

Good salespeople will understand contractual issues and work to understand what the legal terms mean; so, not only can they prepare for finishing a deal all the way through, but they will only enter into contract negotiations once the deal is ready.

Poor salespeople will rush through the sales process so that the deal is not 'cooked' properly and leave large items to be negotiated at the contract stage, which will only end up costing more money and time, since lawyers and others should only be involved when the deal is ready, and all commercial items have been discussed and agreed.

Types of contracts

For some businesses it is quite an easy process to get a signature on some sort of legal document and move forward. It can be quite a short document, such as a purchase order with some standard, rarely negotiated terms of business, or it can be a fixed set of terms and conditions (T&Cs) that resides on a web page, which is referred to in all places necessary. But it is important to have some sort of a legal document in today's world. It needs to encapsulate what will be delivered, what the customer will provide and the key principles of the deal. If this can become a standard set of terms for all customers, then so much the better.

Wherever possible, it is vital that the document is initially drafted and provided by the supplier of goods and services and not the customer. This provides focus on protecting what the supplier deems important. It is a starting point and the parties may largely negotiate around these terms, if there is any negotiation at all. It also helps benchmark how any negotiations are progressing. The documentation should and can be evolved over time to cover situations that relate to the supplier's business. It should be reviewed at regular intervals, even if this is annually. If it is kept reasonable and it doesn't demand anything out of the ordinary, there is no reason why someone shouldn't sign it, and quickly, too.

The documentation should be drafted and checked over by a lawyer experienced in the relevant industry. It makes sense to get a referral to one, if possible. Good lawyers can save a lot of money in the long run, especially as the value of a supplier's company to any purchaser or investor is usually driven by the contracts that have been signed. Bad lawyers, or ones that don't understand the industry, can cost precious time and money.

Larger agreements

For many people, especially in businesses with recurring revenue streams in return for the use of a product or service, it isn't so simple. As the world changes and business models are disrupted and replaced, longer-form contracts are becoming more and more necessary. Legal terms and disclaimers are everywhere these days. Every time someone updates their phone or uses Internet-based services, they are typically asked to sign, or agree to, a set of terms and conditions. Whether they are read or not is optional on a personal level (most people don't read them!), but on a business level management and salespeople should be well versed in them and, if possible, have a good understanding of them.

As a result, more and more businesses are, quite rightly, asking questions of anything they need to sign and choosing to negotiate where they don't agree with certain elements.

If a supplier is going to sell services/products to large companies, they will often have their own legal teams that work across all legal documentation, and salespeople need to be prepared to negotiate and work to understand what their requirements are so that the supplier is not put in a weak position.

Larger companies will also often have their own 'standard' positions on a wide range of legal issues – termination, warrants, indemnities, limitations of liability and so on. Sometimes this is a negotiating ploy in order to start the negotiations off with the supplier in a weak position, and occasionally, these positions are set in stone. Either way, the salespeople should understand enough so that they can work with management and legal professionals to get the deal over the line – or find out quickly if there is no deal to be had.

The best way is for the salesperson to have some sort of 'plain English' document that dictates what has been agreed between them and the customer before the contract comes into play. This lays out all the elements of the deal. If the deal is quite straightforward, then great – it could be an email, for example, that has been agreed with the customer. The simpler the better, as long as it encapsulates all the elements, with no surprises.

For these more complex deals, consider working with 'Heads of Terms', 'Memorandum of Understanding' and 'Letters of Intent', which are all slightly more complicated, but similar ways of agreeing to do business and commercial terms, before moving to expensive and potentially time-consuming longer-form contract negotiations. These are mostly 'non-binding' pending 'binding' legal agreements. Lots of companies make signing a document such as this a prerequisite of entering into long-form contract negotiations.

Getting this document can be a formal part of the sales process – it helps a deal 'pipeline' because salespeople who are confident a deal is done 'bar the paperwork' are often a false hope, despite their optimism. Management should be clear that a deal isn't done until the paperwork is finished.

Many salespeople have trouble getting past this stage and management need to monitor this: firstly, to make sure they can see what may or not be finishing; and, secondly, because they may be able to help.

PROJECTS & ACTIONS

- Decide what sort of legal documentation you think you need. Find a lawyer who understands your business and ethical approach, and discuss these with them. Draft anything first in plain English so the thinking is done on your time, before engaging with a legal professional.
- Build into the sales process and the actions of the salespeople that your organisation will supply legal paperwork to a customer at the appropriate stage.
- For larger deals, require salespeople always to frame the deal and have all commercial terms agreed to *before* entering into potentially long contract negotiations. You could use 'Heads of Terms', 'Memorandum of Understanding' or 'Letters of Intent', or even a simple email exchange, but the document should be sufficiently detailed that a lawyer can draft/modify a contract from it.
- Offer salespeople the ability to learn about the legal documentation they have to get signed and what the fundamental terms mean. It can save lots of money in the future and doesn't have to go too far into the legal detail. There is a blog post on the basic framework of a legal agreement at www.salestribe.blog/legal-agreement-basics
- Be very clear in your sales process which documentation needs to be signed to demonstrate the commitment required from a salesperson. Be very clear that a deal is not finished until the paperwork is signed and any incentives related to signing a deal only get triggered when this happens.
- If you come to the conclusion that your sales process demands that you need to involve a legal professional as part of each deal, make sure you build the cost of that activity into the price of your sale. Lawyers can be expensive. It is also a good idea to provide some incentive

> to a lawyer to help close the deal in a certain time frame –
> maybe through payment terms or a bonus.
> - A handshake goes a long way. Make that the agreement that
>   is brought forward in the paperwork. It is key for credibility.

Negotiating commercial contracts

Many books have been written about negotiation. A deep dive into this subject is beyond the scope of this book but one recommendation would be to read *Never Split the Difference* by Christopher Voss and Tahl Raz. The following is designed to offer some tips in contract negotiation:

- The first principle of negotiation is that it should be approached to try to find a 'win' situation for all parties involved. If the approach from any party involved is just to exploit someone, then it can quickly disintegrate into a situation that won't work.
- Just because the approach should be to find a win, it doesn't necessarily mean compromise. Sticking to principles in place and communicating why it doesn't work to compromise may well be the best approach.
- Negotiation is largely about listening and empathising with the other party. Repeating back to them what someone says often demonstrates that a person is listening, has empathy and can help diffuse difficult situations. Good salespeople will practise and do this.
- Occasionally, a large company may put a set of terms on the table to a small company and insist there will be no negotiation.

At least this makes it a simple choice as to whether or not to go ahead, but it should still be reviewed carefully.

- Approach contract negotiation in a positive manner and uncover what is important for your customer all the way through the process. Negativity in the negotiation process will hinder progress and potentially make it fractious. Smiling is important!

- Preparation is imperative. The salesperson/people should prepare the background of the deal. There should be a plainly worded document that confirms the commercial terms of a deal, and which has been agreed with the customer.

- The basis of negotiation is, hopefully, the contractual terms provided by the supplier organisation. But it may be necessary to use terms provided by the customer. Either way, the first review will usually involve legal professionals and end up with a marked-up document (often called a 'red line'), where one party has marked up the other party's document with the changes they would like to see, to make the agreement or set of terms work for them. This can sometimes be quite extensive but that doesn't mean they are unresolvable.

- Salespeople need to work hard to keep things moving and everyone talking; this is part of their job. Email and other forms of text exchange are often not good during lengthy negotiations and can make problems worse.

- Communication skills are also imperative. It is crucial to ensure the position of the customer is clearly understood, and it helps to regularly boil down the issues into an easy-to-understand list of what needs to be overcome. Listening carefully is the most important skill.

- It is a salesperson's responsibility to understand and be able to communicate clearly what the issues are for each point being negotiated.
- Ultimately, a supplier has to be able to walk away if the deal doesn't work for them. If that attitude is taken into the negotiation, it will come across and often change the dynamics of an engagement. Situations of desperation or of arrogance are equally damaging to a negotiation.
- Great negotiators plan and prepare the negotiations from both their and their counterpart's perspective. Detailed wargaming of your counterpart's position can be invaluable to better understand real strengths and weaknesses.

TIPS & NOTES

Notes on trading

Ultimately, and eventually, the negotiating process will result (hopefully!) in a few items left that are important on both sides. This is where there usually ends up being some trading to make a deal work for both sides. Here are some further notes:

» Even if the contentious items in the documents are discussed point by point, it is not a good idea to try and resolve the bigger stuff in that manner. On larger items, discuss each party's position and understand the situation, then park them as something to revert to at a later stage. This way it may be possible to put a package of contentious issues together and trade them off against a concession on the other side.

» Always try to negotiate from a position of strength.

continued

A salesperson should know where their position is weak and where they may be strong in terms of the things that need to be agreed. Making a list beforehand helps. In the negotiations, the salesperson should choose the items where they are strong and spend time on these wherever possible.

» A first principle in conflict resolution is to find a way to allow the other party a way out which works for both parties. Good salespeople will constantly try and find that.

» For anything big where the customer is worried about being tied to something, one tactic is for the supplier to try and 'de-risk' it for them. For example, reducing the term or providing 'breaks' for non-performance, where customers feel they can get out of a longer-term commitment if it isn't working, can often provide an answer. It can also mean that other contentious issues are no longer contentious because the commitment isn't so great.

» Some issues can be kept on the list that are not that important to the supplier, but are presented as immovable in the negotiations. These should be saved to give up when and if necessary in return for something from the buyer.

» Avoid the negotiations coming down to a single issue and an impasse which puts both sides in a stalemate situation. (If it happens, a break should be scheduled and the issue should be approached from different angles away from the negotiating table.)

» A good negotiator will continually try and understand the other side's position very clearly. This is where really listening is a great skill. Often, seemingly huge issues evaporate, or an easy way around them can be established once the detail has been understood.

» A supplier should decide what is really important to them, but don't give away what that is.

» Slow the process down. Being in a hurry to conclude deals can mean agreeing to things that will be regretted later. When it gets late and it has been a long day, things suddenly seem a lot easier to agree to. A smart negotiating team will plan for that and save energy for it. Setting deadlines for completing deals can put someone in a weak position – discovering the other side's deadlines can often empower the negotiation, even if that is just to go to bed!

» Emotion shouldn't get in the way, but when others exhibit it, it generally means that it may be used to a negotiating advantage to get sticky things agreed. Ultimately, all decisions are driven by some sort of emotion, however small.

» It can be a very dry conversation as lawyers slug it out over points. Salespeople should be responsible for keeping it light and friendly unless there is a major problem. Remember: find all the people who can say 'no' (Chapter 1, Attitude and Approach) – one of them might be the lawyer on the other side!

» Salespeople may be scared that the length of time needed to negotiate will kill the deal, and sometimes that happens. A customer's senior management might be frustrated with the supplier if they are digging their heels in on a point or two, but calmly reminding people that it should be done properly for both sides normally helps. Again, being in a hurry generally means agreeing to things that may be regretted later.

» Don't split the difference. Suggesting meeting in the middle or something similar on a point which has been negotiated hard often seems easier than continuing to discuss it. But particularly in situations where a smaller company is negotiating with a bigger one, this is often not equitable, and can be another source of later regret. Remaining firm and having the energy to negotiate properly to maintain a position that makes sense, with limited concessions, should be the basis of an approach. Why should there be movement?

» If things change substantially in a negotiation, a supplier should be prepared to run its numbers again and work out

continued

whether the deal is still a runner. The rest of the process is irrelevant if everything is given away at the negotiating table and the deal turns into something that doesn't work financially.

» Defer to a higher 'decision maker' if necessary. Top management should be saved for the real showstoppers and not brought into the process until these obstacles are hit. Language such as 'I'm going to take this away and talk to the board about it,' or 'We need to discuss this between us and come back to you,' combined with late-night or long negotiations, can quickly flush out what is important to the other side!

» Make sure what something says is fully understood before it is agreed. The nuances of language are significant in legal documentation and one word can greatly change a meaning. The following shows two 'banana-skin' examples (a good lawyer will explain these and many other nuances):

• 'Reasonable endeavours' means an obligation to act reasonably (as judged by a court of law) to do something but without putting yourself at commercial disadvantage, whereas 'best endeavours' means the obligation is to spend money and do pretty much everything commercially necessary to fulfil that obligation. One word can make a big difference!

• 'Time is of the essence' means that the time you agree will be strictly adhered to, and to the absolute condition of that time. So, if you agree to do something by 12 p.m. on a certain day and 'time is of the essence', then if you haven't done it at 12:01 you are in breach of that agreement.

» Provided you communicate clearly that everything is 'subject to contract', until something is signed it is not agreed. This works both ways: there is no deal until it is signed, but, equally, the things that may be drafted in a document, where others have the expectation that they have been agreed, can still be changed if necessary. It is possible to change things or even walk away right up until that point.

» Good cop, bad cop. This scenario is between two people on the same side. It allows the 'bad cop' to present the worst-case scenario, whereas the 'good cop' will be much more optimistic. The 'bad cop' is generally one of the jobs of the lawyer. It can make the people on the other side agree to a better position for a supplier.

» For major negotiations it is worth running a full rehearsal where half the team conducts the negotiation as if they were your counterpart. You will realise that some of your positioning works well but other parts will open avenues that weaken your position. Rather than make expensive mistakes with your counterpart, refine your approach to ensure you retain maximum control of the negotiation.

Losing a deal

Everyone worked hard, tried everything they could, but it wasn't a success for whatever reason. It isn't a great feeling to lose a deal but sometimes it is the right thing. Good salespeople will conduct a post-mortem and learn as much as they can from this situation, suggest adaptations to the sales process, demonstrations or language used in a sales engagement, since this is often where most may be learned.

PROJECTS & ACTIONS

- Structure a 'deal lost' process that examines elements of why the deal failed without finger pointing. It should be kept high-level where possible but not be so toned down that it doesn't hit the true reasons head-on.
- Failure should be considered a valuable opportunity to learn.
- Adjust the sales process and other elements of the deal-flow to capitalise on the loss.

continued

- Recognise the hard work and effort that went into the process regardless of outcome – often the deals that everyone has worked hard to try and save through complicated negotiations and commitments are the ones that leave people exhausted and with no adrenaline rush of closure.
- Be prepared to revisit a deal later with a prospect. Times, priorities and people change. People may well see the other side in a different light after the heat of battle has subsided and be prepared to revisit on terms that will make them an ideal customer.

Say thank you!

An important part of finishing any deal is saying thank you. A personal note from the management of the company, handwritten where possible, or some other token will not be forgotten. It is important, however, that this really is personal and cuts through the other methods of communication – an email or text message often will not make any impact. It can be a good way of softening the delivery of the first invoice!

10. Metrics, Targets and Measurement

This chapter explores how management of an organisation might set some important metrics as targets and then measure people and efforts against them. It's about effective management over the processes that may be put in place using this book. This chapter is almost exclusively a practical project/exercise in its own right, so no separate ones have been highlighted.

In this chapter we will discuss:
• What should be measured?
• Measurement for new business.
• Helping management focus on the top deals.
• Measuring account management and customer service.

What should be measured?

What we have talked about in this book means nothing without execution through management. Like a general commanding a battalion of troops in battle, execution is vital, often through lots of noise.

An organisation can have the best sales policies and structures in the world, but if the salespeople don't follow them it is unlikely that they will be effective. Sales are about numbers so are ultimately highly measurable. And once an organisation has the data, there are many things that can be done with it.

How does management monitor and manage effectively without it taking up all their time? The answer is to get salespeople to measure themselves and then report back, plus use tools such as a customer relationship management (CRM) system to measure key metrics automatically. This requires organisation and a bit of dedication but, provided there is a clear understanding of *what* is being measured, then there is a plethora of tools that are available to make this increasingly easy for an organisation to implement (see Chapter 7, The Sales Process, CRM systems section). The key is then making sure these tools are used as envisaged – the data coming out is only as good as the data going in – so it is essential that the data is accurate.

Clear measurements, once established, should allow a framework in which everyone understands what they are supposed to do daily, weekly, monthly and so on. It should leave management to fight fires and focus on the end of the sales process, tricky negotiations or the bigger/problem deals that need its assistance. A weekly/monthly/quarterly review of the metrics and an ongoing tally each month/quarter/year can provide the organisation with great insights, especially when coupled with the sales process (see Chapter 7).

It's best to keep the metrics simple. If they are too complicated they will cause arguments and won't be an effective way of measuring.

No one should be too senior to sign up to relevant metrics. It can be made part of a wider human resources policy since hitting these metrics should be 'SMART' – Specific, Measurable, Achievable, Relevant, Timely.

You are what you measure

Dan Ariely is Professor of Psychology and Behavioural Economics at Duke University, Durham, North Carolina, and a founding member of the Center for Advanced Hindsight. He wrote an article in the *Harvard Business Review* in 2010 entitled 'You Are What You Measure', whose key message was that whatever metrics and measurements you put in place, they are the things that will end up most influencing your business. His article used the example of CEOs and the influence of company share price on their day-to-day activity. If they are measured on this one metric, then they will do everything to affect that metric in their daily actions to the detriment of all other activity.

The same is true of salespeople, so it is important to form the metrics that are required not only to measure elements of the sales process, but also to influence the behaviour of the individual/team to support an organisation's sales activity – and these can be refined and adjusted over time if they yield a negative activity.

Measurement for new business

These are some of the things to consider and why. These metrics should be clearly linked to steps in the sales process (Chapter 7). Wherever possible, 'dashboards' should be created in the CRM to monitor these metrics.

An example: number of phone calls made 58; target 100; achieved 58 per cent.

1. Number of calls made/period. It is easy to record this and makes a very basic and effective sales metric. 'Calls' can mean phone calls, emails, meetings, etc. All of the above.
2. Number of phone calls over x minutes in length. It is easy to make phone calls, but what quality are they? The content should be captured somewhere in notes to back this up.
3. Number of face-to-face sales meetings had. As we have discussed, this is where the important stuff is usually done, so it is important that there is a regular flow. Don't forget to check the notes that are being made!
4. Number of people met within an organisation. Meeting more people is important to find all those who can say 'no' to a deal. Track who they are – influencer, decision maker, management, junior, etc. Perhaps build an org chart for an important large deal?
5. Number of attendees invited to an event, and number that attended. Establishing a supplier as experts through running events will mean this is important.

6. Number of new contacts input. Contact data for new suspects and prospects is captured.

7. Number of units sold or deals completed. Only applicable if you target on this basis.

8. Revenue number sold. Normally the most important thing, but different from the above – having a salesperson who only brings small-ticket items when the organisation wants to sell large ones could be monitored.

9. Gross profit of sales. Another key metric for some.

10. Gross margin (GM) achieved. There is no point making a lot of revenue if GM targets haven't been achieved.

11. Number of discounts applied for. This can be very important because it shows you that salespeople are being competitive. If no one has given a discount, it generally means that the pricing hasn't been competitive enough in a deal-making situation versus the competition.

12. Number of leads followed up on. You can also capture the lead sources here if they are relevant: calls, social media, email, events, etc.

13. Number of conversions from lead to prospective customer. What is the quality of the leads you are generating and how many are you being able to convert to the beginning of the sales process? If you see swings in either direction, it tells you how your marketing effort is performing. But how these then convert from that point to becoming a prospective customer will determine how the beginning of your sales funnel is operating.

14. Number of prospects reaching 25/50/90 per cent of sales process/pipeline/funnel MTD/QTD/YTD. You can see

the movement by reviewing the deal-flow and what the shift is.

15. Conversion rate at each stage of the process. Monitor to see if a salesperson is able to convert from lead to prospective customer well, but isn't able to develop a deal further. Similarly, if someone can finish deals well, but is unable to take the customer on the initial engagement with the process, maybe some adjustment to skill set is needed.

16. Overall conversion rate from lead generation to close. How many deals come from the leads that are generated? In reverse this informs management how leads need to be generated, of a certain quality, that reach x stage in the process to yield y number of deals.

17. Revenue from deals lost total and at each stage that matters.

18. Year-to-date (YTD), quarter-to-date (QTD) selection of the above (or all of them). It's good to keep a total tally.

19. Competition encountered. You need to monitor deals done and new entrants to your market. Also note how long a contract is likely to be so you can revisit.

20. Number of events/lunches/drinks bought or attended. This is not a joke and should mean something – lunches and drinks can be as good as a decent sales presentation. They may not yield something immediately tangible, but they may support bolstering the opinion of influencers and decision makers. Or they may be a total waste of time and money.

Once recording this information is set up and made the relevant people's responsibility to pull it together or record it, it should become second nature to use it.

Usually, a sales call is held once a week to examine obstacles and barriers which salespeople are encountering where these metrics are discussed. It is important to use these calls to allow salespeople to communicate to one another and generate competition by comparing them with one another – it can be a great motivator.

This, coupled with a regular monthly one-on-one meeting with each salesperson in which the metrics are reviewed, alongside the sales process (Chapter 7), should provide all that is needed to monitor and execute.

Helping management focus on the top deals

Part of the reporting activity to management should provide the ability to focus on finishing a deal. As discussed in the sales process (Chapter 7), management should be focused largely on the end of the process. When a review of deal-flow (pipeline/funnel) is conducted, it would seem that all the best deals will be at the end, or the nearest to being finished, but sometimes it isn't so clear. Occasionally, even if a deal is not so far through the sales process, it can still be something that management and other parts of the company need to focus on. This is where salespeople should tell management which they think are the top deals that they will bring to the organisation at any one time. A simple marker in the CRM system can identify these and they should be discussed at every sales meeting.

One way of achieving this is to hold a bi-weekly meeting (or call) in which each new business person prepares a list of up to five of their top deals, what products/services they are for (if applicable), how much they are worth and what the obstacles are to closing them. It doesn't have to be five, it could be twenty (or two), as long as it is relevant, to the point and provides a clear list of focus points for management.

TIPS & NOTES

Focusing on top deals should not be limited to new business alone. A successful organisation will persistently look for deals with its existing customers, and these may be even more lucrative. It is important in a lot of cases that these are examined in the same way as new business.

Measuring account management and customer service

The account management or customer-service function generally deals with existing customers (see Chapter 11). Expanding a relationship with those customers can have a similar measurement style as the new business approach, provided it is treated as a commercial activity. So it is necessary to develop a similar set of metrics for existing customer deal pipeline as given above for new business. However, some additional key metrics should be added. Here is a suggestion of the top ones:

1. Number of contact points, how many times and on what topic. How high-maintenance is the customer to the supplier organisation? How busy are the account managers looking after the customer? These can be outbound or inbound communications. Categorise the topics so that trends can be seen developing. If communication is solely via email, this should be reviewed and maybe changed.

2. New opportunities with customer. These need a value on them as soon as possible and can be presented in the deal-flow document or equivalent, alongside their relevant stage in the sales process.

3. A list of customers with no visible sales opportunity: is there a way to establish one?

4. Last social interaction with customer. These days, there are some strict guidelines for anti-bribery laws and so on, especially around excessive levels of entertainment. However, it is very important that a level of social interaction is maintained between people in both organisations. This should be supported by a budget and should involve other parts of both organisations apart from just the sales team/management; the same should apply on the customer's side. The more ingrained a supplier can be in the thoughts and minds of its customer, the better customers it will usually have.

5. Top five issues in the last month that have affected commercial relationship. It doesn't have to be five, but up

to five. This is important so as to see trends developing across a business that can be fixed.

6. Key wins in the last three months. Key deals that the person/team has brought over the line in the last three months.

7. Potential hotspots and fires. A smart supplier will try as much as possible to be proactive and not reactive to customer issues – act on something before it arrives. If management sees something on the horizon it should be acted upon in advance, where possible, or at least there should be a plan for what might happen when it hits.

8. What is the number one issue affecting a customer? Customers are one of the most important areas of market feedback. This information should be used to inform management and the rest of the company how a customer's business is doing. This can be used to identify new products and innovations outside the scope of existing products and services.

If a 'star partners' programme (see Chapter 11, on account management) or similar is adopted to work with an organisation's top customers, then adjusting the metrics, or having additional ones, may be required in order to make sure these customers are being looked after in a particularly special way. For example, adding some sort of measurement of where the supplier organisation has delivered them particular value, and how that can be worked to recognise them. Their status as a 'star partner' should also be monitored through defined metrics.

Measuring competition

A supplier can use competition to help measure where it should be. It should monitor them closely and establish some metrics around which it can benchmark its company and product or service offerings.

1. Keep a database on each competitor and ensure that it is someone's job to keep this up to date from all the relevant sources that are available.

2. Monitor all the numbers, new customer signings and any key launches or new/enhanced product announcements.

3. Closely monitor changes in their value proposition, pricing changes they may make and any innovations in customer service or support around their products and services.

4. Closely monitor their new staff appointments and changes in personnel. When changes start taking place in a company, it is often true that the people who work there don't like it and might be ready for a change. Interviewing a competition's sales staff is often a very good way to find out what is happening there. If people leave a company, then it is often a great time to have lunch or a coffee with them.

5. Tools such as LinkedIn and Google Alerts can make monitoring competition a lot easier. It is amazing what sometimes key employees in an organisation are allowed to publish on social media channels to advertise their expertise. A smart supplier will also monitor its organisation to make sure it is not doing the same!

11. Looking After Existing Customers

The world is increasingly customer-driven. Looking after customers is of paramount importance. Account support/ management or 'farming' and nurturing a relationship can often lead to the greatest potential growth. There is often a 'Pareto principle' regarding existing customers where 80 per cent of the revenues will come from 20 per cent of existing customers.

In the Information Age more and more companies are trying to adopt a business model which has a recurring-revenue stream paid by customers in return for a product or ongoing service, or an element of them.

For a lot of businesses, significant growth in relationships with existing customers can be more realistic than selling to new customers. After all, if they already fit an ideal customer profile, expanding a relationship should be a critical focus.

And for some businesses, simple ways can be found to add additional revenue opportunities without 'hard sell' (see page 230 – 'Commercialising customer service').

In this chapter we will discuss:

- Putting the customer at the centre of focus.
- The sales process for existing customers.
- Commercialising the customer service and management function.
- Management, customer service and account management reporting.
- Distribution, aggregators, affiliates and other strategic relationships.
- Sacking a customer.
- Star customers/partners.

Putting the customer at the centre of focus

A unique account management and customer-service process, tailored for a company, should be developed to help the business succeed. The account management process should put the customer at the centre of the picture across the whole organisation – something a lot of people say, but rarely do. It can give an organisation an edge over the competition and make happy and positive relationships which end up being more like business partnerships than just supplier/buyer relationships.

A REAL-LIFE EXAMPLE

In one business, our revenue derived from the success of our customers: if they did well offering our product to their customers, then we did well; if they didn't do well with our product, they would most likely do well with other suppliers and we would suffer. We were a small company and had to be very focused on this element.

Our products were games used by our customers on their websites and mobile applications by their own customers. In other words, the more attractive our product was and the better it was understood by our customers, the better they would promote it, the more our customers clients would pay to use it and the more money we would earn from it.

Ours was a very high-quality product, but we didn't know before it was launched to the market how well it would be received by the end-customers – the customers of our customers. Our account management function is what delivered this data to us and continually influenced the parts of the company which needed to respond to the customer's needs.

The approach

The team we had to service our customers had to be able to think as if they were in the shoes of the person running our section of the business within the customer. Most of our customers had upwards of forty suppliers, usually managed by a small team inside the customer and sometimes one individual. The revenues earned from this part of the business were usually significant for the main business of the customer, so there was a good focus on it as part of the overall picture.

But these people were very busy and to 'cut through' it meant we had to focus on them, and continually find the problems they were going through and the challenges they were facing. If we hadn't found these, our competition would have, and the customers would have gravitated towards them.

We were never able to assign one person to each customer since the revenues didn't warrant it, but we could make it a process where our account management team was able to give the right information to a customer for them to make informed choices and make their lives easier. Over time these choices would also make it easier for them to promote our products heavily. Here is how we structured it:

- *We insisted that our whole team, not just the salespeople, were a pleasure to deal with and most of our customers appreciated that. We were happy, positive and ready for engagement, proving that working together, through sometimes difficult issues, needn't be something that couldn't be positive and rewarding.*
- *We made sure we were professional and passionate: we were well prepared for all meetings and calls, we had done our homework and knew what to recommend and what to push without being a*

hard sell. We adopted a familiar format for each encounter which gave our take on the state of the relationship and the market, whether this was a pack of information, a single sheet or snippet of information. Where there were numbers regarding performance (which there would always be if possible), they were accurate and didn't conflict with the customer's own data.

- *We knew our product inside and out: it was our job to know the product better than the customer and we would be on hand to offer recommendations and answer questions on the finer details of our product or services. We could also demonstrate new enhancements or new product innovation provided by our company where possible, and discuss how the product might help the customer solve a problem or fill an opportunity we may have identified as part of our relationship with them.*

- *We knew the market. Most importantly, without giving away confidential information, we were able to offer advice and tricks and tips from the market to make the most from our product. How to market a particular feature, where to put certain marketing elements on a website for maximum engagement, and so on.*

- *We knew which of our products were doing well across all our customers and something about why. We would actively tell our customers which of our products were good and which were not so* good. This meant that everyone focused on the best product set we could produce.

- Our account management people saw themselves as the representative of the customer within our business. So considerable empathy was received by the customer and it made us able to prioritise based on proper feedback.

- We had an escalation process which allowed any seemingly major issues to be dealt with quickly. It is important to have a proactive customer relationship so that any issues are dealt with as soon as possible and not left to grow into major storms – a lot of 'storms in teacups' get dealt with very easily this way. Picking up the phone or meeting face to face is very important these days and often it is about your company being the one to 'cut through' and make that phone call rather than hitting 'reply' to an email. We also had a programme which meant that there was regular contact in more social environments: lunches, coffees and so on.

- We were experts in our business. We continued to learn, share and make mistakes with our customers as their businesses responded to market forces, which were changing rapidly. We helped them compete more effectively by understanding their business better over time. We allowed them access to our best product people to work with them to influence product or even build product for them specifically for a period.

- *Our company culture was one of everyone being customer-focused without letting them distract us too much. This is often a fine balance, particularly when you have a very demanding customer. The general attitude of all the people at the company was one of excellent customer service. This is really important – if everyone is continually challenging and second-guessing the customer's credentials, it definitely comes across and creates a lot of negativity.*

- *Our aim was to make the people we dealt with in our customer's organisation look great and hit their targets. This made their lives and their relationships with their colleagues and management better. In turn, this made them more likely to want to deal with us over our competition.*

- *Even if your revenue doesn't come from the business success of your customer, you should still treat them as if it does.*

PROJECTS & ACTIONS

- Consider how to adapt the above example to your business. How do you put the customer at the centre and what changes need to be made to have that working?
- What systems and processes will you put in place to monitor that each is happening? Notes in the CRM system? Data from financial people? Product training from product people? Events with specific members of the team and customer representatives?
- Consider having a day a week or month where you mutually agree that all communication between your

---

continued

customer's staff and your staff is only done verbally before anything is written into an email.

- There should be a regularly scheduled conversation between the salesperson or people and the customer which deals with certain sales elements. The frequency of the meetings and who should be at them should be set in advance. Even if there is daily dialogue between a supplier's team and the customer's, there should still be regular scheduled meetings or events where a detailed look is made into some key metrics, agreed upon by both the supplier and the customer. Generating these metrics is a reason to engage in this regular dialogue, which will generally yield much more than just a review of some numbers.

- For larger accounts, a regular 'high-level' meeting may make sense, to which more senior people are invited from both sides and at which more strategic or direction-based items are discussed. It is now quite common for people to have Quarterly Business Reviews (QBRs) at a senior level.

  a. These meetings should have tight agendas with individually owned parts to them: if it is the responsibility of a team to execute some actions, agree a point person on each side who takes that responsibility. Collective responsibility is often an excuse for inaction.

  b. Extensive notes should be taken and distributed to all, with clear times by which the actions should be completed and whose responsibility they are. Otherwise, there is little point in having any meetings. These actions should be regularly reviewed and followed up. Any that aren't completed should be reviewed again and either carried forward or discarded by mutual consent.

- The data presented in any communication should be accurate and relevant. Some analysis should be done on the data that shows trends or findings of genuine interest. The account management function should be able to retrieve this data from other parts of the company (with or without assistance) and be capable of performing the analysis itself. If this is complicated, tools should be made available to them.

- How will the sales team run the relationship and what regular touch points will they have with the customer? Who is responsible for organising those and making sure they happen? Who is responsible for capturing actions and making sure they are followed up on?
- What data and insights will your commercial people give that supports the increase in business? Which supports uncovering different problems and how they may be solved?
- Adapt your sales process for new business to deal with additional business coming from existing customers.
- One way of measuring the success of the staff who look after your customers is to ask them to complete a regular (quarterly?) performance review.

The sales process for existing customers

Adding a new product or service to an existing arrangement should follow a similar process to the new business sales process (see Chapter 7). There are some elements that should already be in place: for example, a confidential environment should already be established, problems that can be fixed should be easier to uncover and so on.

But when there is an existing customer relationship, there should also be a process in place for how regular dialogue should be approached in day-to-day relations and outside of any major customer service or operational issues. This can change depending on the customer, but with the same basic principles for all to help manage them.

Commercialising the customer service and management function

It is quite easy to end up with a situation where those assigned to support existing businesses only focus on that support function and not necessarily on selling more product or service offerings to an existing customer. That is fine for some businesses, but for others this should be a key place to focus on sales aspects and try to upsell new products and enhancements. If a supplier sells, invoices and delivers a product to a customer, and little or no support is required, it probably makes sense to keep the responsibility for selling the product and any others within a new business sales approach and have support staff that are not sales-oriented in any way.

However, it is increasingly normal to use this function as an important touch point for additional new revenue streams or sales opportunities. For these, instead of using new business sales capabilities, which should be focused on hunting for new deals, it may be preferable to establish a way to utilise the people who are running the account management or customer services function to bring this business to a company.

As discussed in Chapter 2, Basic Types of Sales Roles and How to Fill Them, people suited to account management or support-staff-type roles are often not those who are aggressive hunters of new business, although there are always exceptions to any rule. But this can be made to work in favour of a supplier.

PROJECTS & ACTIONS

- Look for simple ways to add revenue-earning opportunities to daily interaction with customers without 'hard sell'. See anecdote below.

- Set the expectation that the people in certain roles are responsible for bringing and upselling or uplifting revenues through their activities.

- At a minimum, provide a feedback mechanism for anyone involved with customer touch points to be able to give a steer where they believe there is a sales opportunity.

- Have clear targets for each individual (see Chapter 10, Metrics, Targets and Measurements) and some kind of reward for hitting those targets. Commission can be used here but consider other incentives as discussed in Chapter 3). Participation in a bonus scheme or some kind of non-monetary incentive which has value (for example: holiday, dinner/lunch with significant others) is also a good motivator.

- It is always good to create some sort of competition between people if possible. It helps with banter, can create real tension and ultimately can even be fun!

COMMERCIALISING CUSTOMER SERVICE

Most people have car windscreens replaced through their insurance policy. The insurance company usually has a preferred auto glass company which is dealt with to get the windscreen replaced. Most of this can be achieved through a fairly 'frictionless process', without talking to a human being, until you arrive at the service centre or they come to fix the windscreen. If an excess is payable, this is usually collected by the auto glass company, which creates a transactional relationship between them and the customer. Winning the contract with the insurance companies is a highly competitive area of business where margins will be squeezed to a bare minimum.

So how can the glass company turn this situation into a simple upsell opportunity that their friendly representatives can be trusted to perform, even though they are not 'salespeople'? Where can they add extra revenues from the customer outside their arrangement with the insurance company? What can they sell that is simple to install, easy to carry for the road technicians, but a high-quality product with good margin?

A lot of people have wear and tear on their windscreen wipers and never think about replacing them until they fail a suitable test. Since the glass company is replacing the windscreen, they are working on that part of the car already and checking the performance of the wipers is a simple process. It should be easy to demonstrate to a customer that they need a new set of wipers. Once volumes are high, the glass company can command a good price to buy the wiper blades – some of which they can pass on to the customer. This means the customer gets a good deal, continues to appreciate the quality of their brand-new windscreen when it is wet and doesn't have the hassle of getting it replaced at a later date. The glass company has added a high-margin activity to a potential low-margin one and turned the Information Age to work in its favour.

Management, customer service and account management reporting

Management usually needs to be close to customers. In any business where management is not, customer satisfaction is bound to suffer and, as a result, potential sales opportunities are lost. In addition, if management is not close to a company's customers it cannot be close to the market. Obviously, customer-service people are the front line here, but there should be clear, regular reporting to management (monthly at least) on the status of each regular or recurring customer, in a digestible form, especially for the top customers and, if possible, all relevant ones. This should report key highlights in the relationship with the customer (launches, concerns, etc.), the main metrics and data on the performance of the customer, projects that are ongoing and their status, as well as clear sales objectives and their status. It is also an opportunity to spot ongoing trends in the business and in competitors, which are also included in the metrics. This is essential for keeping up with change in the market as it happens.

There should also be clearly defined levels of escalation for each issue that may arise that affect the sales status of the customer.

Distribution, aggregators, affiliates and other strategic relationships

Distribution, aggregators, affiliates and other strategic relationships need looking after and nurturing in their own specific ways, especially if a supplier is new to the market or product area.

For the staff working in these organisations, it may be that they receive some sort of bonus or commission for selling a supplier's product. As an example, 'sales performance incentive fund' (SPIF) events are when you have a certain time/day when a distribution agent gets to push a supplier's products, and that supplier gives a bonus directly to the salesperson of the distribution company for any sales that are made. This can be cash or other incentives pre-agreed with the management.

Aggregation partners and affiliates embody relationships driven through specific marketing arrangements and can drive a significant amount of business the way of a supplier if they are set up and run well. Usually, however, it is down to the nuances of the specific market, which is why the account-support functions should be involved to help monitor and massage the relationships here for maximum gain.

Margin should be continually monitored to keep these relationships profitable and explore their true worth. It is easy to get into a situation where a relationship is established which gives great value early on, but this doesn't last beyond this early stage.

Strategic relationships with other vendors through 'value-added reseller' (VAR) partners, where a supplier's product or service can be put together with another's to provide more value and a complementary package, can be highly lucrative. Care should be taken, however, that a supplier's value is clearly recognised in the deals. The account-support or management role here is to maintain communication and monitor the elements of the deal so that they yield the maximum amount possible and a product line is well represented. If potential customers receive a product or service through a third party and it is substandard, it can tarnish a reputation.

Sacking a customer

Inevitably, any organisation will reach a stage where they have customers who are both good and bad. People's businesses change and so do their requirements of a supplier. They may have been a major challenge from the outset. A supplier's business changes, too. Whatever the situation, it is sometimes necessary for management to consider whether discontinuing a relationship is better for the supplier organisation than continuing a bad one. Indeed, it can make a massive difference if resources are spent on a relationship that is incompatible between organisations.

Important considerations to be made here:
- Does a customer still fit the ideal customer profile outlined in Chapter 5?
- Is the customer more disruptive than the value the supplier is getting from the relationship?
- Does the customer pay on time?
- How much money is it costing to service the customer? This can be intangible but can usually be measured.

- Does the customer still continue to fulfil commitments to a project for a product or service to reach its full potential?
- What is the reputational effect on continuing a relationship? Is this hampering and affecting new business efforts in the marketplace through unfair negative feedback?

PROJECTS & ACTIONS

- Put a monitoring system in place which examines the relationship versus commitments made. Make it a part of the account management responsibility to not only review star partners (see below) but the opposite.
- Remember that contracts are not supposed to be bandages for bad relationships – it is possible to negotiate anything, and staying in a bad relationship or even a business area could seriously affect a business's ability to survive.
- Wherever possible, deal with a broken relationship in a similar way to how you might an employee who is disruptive and talk to the customer about it first. Then, if things don't improve, issue some sort of warning or let them know that things cannot continue as they are.
- For situations where a relationship is governed by orders, make the payment terms really unattractive or create some sort of impact that can make a disruptive customer stop ordering, or at least force a change in the relationship.
- Just as you were able to say 'no' in the run-up to a deal in the sales process without appearing arrogant, so you should be able to be able to say 'no' to continuing a relationship which isn't working. Communicate firmly and fairly exactly why.
- It is very easy for a customer to blame suppliers for their own faults. It is possible to find that the customer changes things significantly when they realise that a supplier no longer wants to be a part of their business, so you may end up losing all the hassle and none of the business.

Star customers/partners

All customers are *not* equal! Despite anyone's best efforts, there will usually be some great customers, some that are not so great and some that turn out to be very different from the perception of them when they went through the sales process.

Consideration should be given to making a number of customers 'star customers'; perhaps five to ten of them. These are normally, but not always, the largest customers for a business in terms of revenue/profit. There could also be a customer who brings a significant strategic opportunity, but the initial revenues are small, and so on.

Star customers/partners are made known to an entire business and to the most important customers, with a clear message that if a task is undertaken for them, or if they see a communication from them, this should be treated as a priority within their own workload.

A customer becoming a star partner shouldn't be a decision that is made by the customer but by the management of the supplier. It is not something that will be added to a contract to bind a supplier to it – it should be based on a set of tangible and intangible metrics, and not necessarily just how much money someone is making.

PROJECTS & ACTIONS

- Determine how a 'star customer' will be identified. Set a regular time to review who these customers are and if they should stay on the list. If you find you are changing the list a lot, you may have a problem, which you need to look into regarding the quality of the relationships. It should rarely change if you are building decent long-term relationships with your customers.

- Communicate to each customer that they are a 'star customer' as it will help you to show them you are taking the relationship seriously; but if for any reason that customer is removed from the list, you need to be able to explain why without destroying the existing relationship.

The Future

The future contains a disrupted path for a lot of professions. Doctors, for example, face the very real fact that their jobs will rely on technology and machines empowered by a massive amount of data coupled with artificial intelligence (AI). It will mean a lot of decisions are no longer made by them. Medical general practitioners by their nature are increasingly more reliant on this flow of information and for 'gates' provided by technology and data in their processes to trap mistakes they may make. While it is unlikely that the technology and automated decision making will always be 100 per cent accurate for some time, it will certainly rapidly change the way generalists operate. In this case, are they really actually doctors as we know them today?

Non-general specialists in the medical profession will also have access to a vast array of data and the recommendation engines of today will probably evolve into empowered decision-making tools that could mean all but the most niche medical areas are automated.

For sales, there is a similar picture. However, the bar is likely to be set in a different place. Yes, generalists will face (and already are facing) a world where technology, 'big data' and AI will change their jobs or make them relatively 'unskilled'. For this reason, sales in the business-to-consumer (B2C) world as a skill is more likely to disappear quickly – this is already happening in some sectors such as insurance, travel and utilities.

But buying something is an emotional exercise, and as long as buyers are human, it is unlikely that they will want to buy things above a certain level of complexity through dealing only with a machine. The extent to which it can be automated will be determined for each industry and situation. But in complex business-to-business (B2B) and more niche B2C areas, it is unlikely that selling will ever be completely replaced, unless the transaction is between machines.

Deal-making can often come from nothing obvious. Someone still needs to evaluate a situation and think about better ways of solving a problem to suit a potential buyer. AI may ultimately be able to present the options, but the nuances involved in situations are often more complicated on a human level. Personalities come into play and those are specific to individuals, groups and situations.

And, yes, the resultant agreement may then be stored in some sort of technology that captures a much more reproduceable set of intentions than a written document. But someone still needs to get the deal to contract stage in order for the terms to be encapsulated in that way.

More likely, and unless the world only has a few companies or organisations that control all of the business, is that non-generalist salespeople get empowered by the tools, technology and data that are available to them to enable them to do their jobs better.

The organisations that will succeed will be the ones that can learn to use the technology, data and AI to be able to create opportunities and craft deals more effectively. These companies will allow themselves to adapt their products and services based on this market intelligence and be able to reflect the diversity of their customers in their sales teams.

But these organisations will also need to have some fundamental clarity around their approach, culture and base values in order to maximise their use of the tools through their people in the right way as opportunities are generated or come along.

Provided this approach is correct, the Information Age is one where sales can really deliver success for any organisation.

Index

account management 8, 55–8, 63,
65, 68, 70, 78, 79, 110, 194, 209,
222–30, 233, 236
    account manager characteristics
        57–8, 63, 65, 68, 77, 79, 230
    account manager incentives 77
    account manager recruiting 57–9
    function of 55–8
    measuring 209, 216–18
    putting the customer at the
        centre of focus 55–7, 70,
        222–9
    reporting 233, 236
advertising 96, 171–2
aggregators 173–4, 222, 233–4
attitude and approach 13–41

blogging 8, 31, 36, 61, 64, 67, 96, 100,
    109, 134, 155, 164, 165, 166, 167,
    179, 183, 200, 249
business development 52–5, 63, 66,
    67–8
buying lists 170–1, 185

cheap, being too 105, 121–2
closed questions 136–7
cold calling 185–6
commercial contracts 195, 201–3
commercial customer service 55–7
commission 7, 48, 51, 71–9, 115, 196,
    231, 234
    disincentives 71, 73–4, 75

incentivising desired activity 71,
    74–5
    performance and 71–3
    structuring 71, 75–7
    why pay? 71–3
committed prospect 147–8
competition 15, 30, 38, 77, 83, 89,
    92, 105, 107, 110, 111, 112, 113,
    188, 191, 213, 214, 215, 222, 224,
    227, 231
    lead generation and 168
    market knowledge and 90–1
    measuring 219
    price and 40–1, 114, 115–16,
        117, 118
conclusion/decision ('Obtaining
    Commitment') 133–4
conferences 27, 33
    expertise recognition and 95–6
    launches and 97–8
    lead generation and 169–70
    market knowledge and 88–9
    tactics for 187–8
confidence 15, 29–32, 47, 48, 63, 65,
    67, 68, 159
contracts 34, 78, 113, 120, 124, 148,
    169, 195, 214, 231–2, 236, 237, 240
    negotiating commercial 195,
        201–7
    salespeople's attitude to signing
        196
    types of 197–201

conversations with prospective and existing customers 97

customer
commercial customer service 55–7
commercialising the customer service function 222, 230–2
conversations with 97
customer relationship management (CRM) system 7, 25, 86, 130, 131, 145, 154–5, 164, 210
customer service reporting 233
end-customer 89–90, 192, 223
likely 144, 148–9
looking after existing 221–38
market knowledge and 86, 89–90
measuring 216–18
pipeline or funnel (list of potential deals) 11, 16, 17, 25, 129, 143, 199–200, 213–14, 215, 217
price and see price
profile, ideal 11, 32, 99–104
prospect (organisation that has been through a set of qualification questions and fits an organisation's ideal customer profile) 11, 14, 16, 17, 22, 26, 30, 49, 65, 66, 99, 101, 110, 127, 140, 144, 146, 147–8, 153, 166, 177, 208
putting at the centre of focus 222–9
sacking a 222, 235–6
sales process and see sales
star 222, 237–8
suspect (organisation that on the surface could be a potential customer but has not been matched to the seller's ideal customer profile) 11, 22, 49, 65, 66, 99, 101, 144, 145, 166

deals
commercial contracts, negotiating 195, 201–3
contracts see contracts
finishing 195–208
how many are out there 13, 17–19
losing 207–8
management focus on top 215–16
trading and 203–7
defensible pricing 105, 120
definitions 11, 32
demographic considerations 101–4
de-risking 105, 112–13
detail, attention to 24
discount 105, 119–20, 127, 192, 213
disincentives 71, 73–4, 75
distribution 173–4, 222, 233–5

effort and energy 36–9
elevator pitches 157, 158–61, 178, 182, 186
email 179–83
empathy, developing 13, 23–4, 50, 58, 64, 141, 180, 201, 226
end-customer 89–90, 192, 223
engage 157–94
cold calling by phone 185–7
elevator pitches 157, 158–61
email 179–85
entertainment 189
lead generation 157, 163–75
networking 178–9
practise 161
retail companies and procurement departments 157, 191–3
selling when there is no active process 157, 162
targeting 157, 175–7
tenders and RFxs 189–90

Index

trade show and conferences
    187–8
entertainment 189
events 88–9, 94–6, 97–8, 169–70,
    178, 183, 186, 187–9, 212, 213,
    214, 227, 228, 234
expert, becoming an 81–98
    blogging and social media 96
    characteristics of an expert 81,
        82–3
    competition and 90–1
    components that make up
        expertise 81, 83–92
    conference and press circuit 95–6
    conferences and exhibitions 88–9
    conversations with prospective
        and existing customers 97
    end-customer view 89–90
    fake it till you make it 97
    market knowledge 83, 85–92
    people knowledge 91–2
    press and PR 86–7
    product launch at an event 97–8
    product or service knowledge
        83–5
    prospective customers and
        existing customers 86
    public information 87–8
    recognised, how to get a
        company's expertise 81, 93–8
    trends 90
    website 93–4
    workshops, events and
        presentations 94–5

fake it till you make it 97
farming (account management)
    55–8, 221
finishing a deal 64, 68, 76, 188,
    195–208
    commercial contracts, negotiating
        195, 201–3
    losing a deal 195, 207–8

salespeople's attitude to signing
        contracts 195, 196
    thank you, saying 208
    trading 203–7
    types of contracts 195, 197–202
future, the 239–41

hiring 5, 43, 44–5, 59, 60, 61, 64, 68,
    72, 92
    account manager 57–70
    business developers 52–5
    holding out for the right person
        58–9
    hunter/'closer' 47–50
    interview questions 60–70
    pre-sales/'opener' 50–2
    sales account management 55–7
    sales roles 43–70
hunter, the/'closer' 47–50, 51, 52, 56,
    65, 66, 67, 68, 72, 75, 230

implication questions 138, 139, 143
inbound marketing 155, 166, 171
incentivising desired activity 71,
    74–5
interview questions 60–70
introduction ('Preliminaries'), sales
    process and 132
is there a fit? ('Demonstrating
    Capability'), sales process and
    133

lead generation 145, 155, 157,
    163–75, 214
    advertising 171–2
    buying lists 170–1
    competition 168
    distributors/aggregators 173–4
    events 169–70
    finding people to engage with
        163–5
    generation areas 165–75
    outside your network 166–7

press and public relations 173
referrals 168–9
retargeting 172
software tools 166–7
ten lead generation areas 165–75
trade press databases 167
websites and social media
    destinations 165–6
likely customer 144, 148–9
listening 20–1, 23, 24, 25, 36, 44, 45,
    50, 62, 64, 65, 69, 140, 158, 179,
    182, 186, 201, 203, 204
losing a deal 195, 207–8

management, account see account
    management
market knowledge 83, 85–92
    competition 90–1
    conferences and exhibitions 88–9
    end-customer and 89–90
    people knowledge 91–2
    press and PR 86–7
    prospective customers and
        existing customers 86
    public information 87–8
    trends 90
metrics, targets and measurement
    209–19
    account management and
        customer service, measuring
        209, 216–18
    competition, measuring 209, 219
    helping management focus on the
        top deals 209, 215–16
    new business measurement 209,
        212–15
    what should be measured 209–11
monitoring sales 149
Most-Favoured Nations principle
    106, 122–4, 191
motive, sales process and uncovering
    ('Investigating') 132–3

need-payoff questions 139, 142, 143
negotiating
    commercial contracts 195, 201–7
    trading and 203–7
networking 69, 91, 100, 102
    events 178–9
    lead generation and 163–5
new business see sales

objections, sales and 141–3
open questions 136–7
opportunities/fallbacks, sales and
    144, 145

people knowledge 91–2
persistence
    golden 32–5
    intelligent 32–5, 44, 47, 66,
        141–2, 162, 163, 186
pipeline or funnel (list of potential
    deals) 11, 16, 17, 25, 129, 143,
    199–200, 213–14, 215, 217
pitch 25–9, 66, 70, 94–5, 162, 181,
    182, 186, 188
    elevator pitches 157, 158–61, 178,
        182, 186
    how and when (and when not)
        to 25–7
    networking and 178
    treating people as human 27–8
practise, engagement 161
pre-sales/'opener' 50–2, 100, 184
presentations 10, 23, 26, 27, 28–9, 35,
    48, 66, 89, 94–5, 135, 158, 214
press and PR, market knowledge and
    86–7, 173
pricing 7, 10, 18, 22, 68, 83, 89,
    105–27, 135, 142, 147, 151, 152,
    153, 154, 166, 190, 191, 192, 193,
    200, 213, 219
    cheap, being too 105, 121–2
    de-risking and determining the
        price 105, 112–13

defensible 105, 120
determining 105, 113–17
discount 105, 119–20
introducing 126–7
Most-Favoured Nations and
    similar value killers 122–4
profitability and 114, 115
raising 43
selling on price 13, 40–1
setting 122
shopping on price alone 117–19
simple or complicated 124–6
value and 105, 107–12
worth, assessing 105, 106–7
problem questions 137–8, 143
problems, uncovering 13, 20–3
procurement departments 32, 157,
    176, 190, 191–4
product
    knowledge 83–5
    launch 97–8
profitability, pricing and 114, 115
proposal, sales process and 151–3
prospect (organisation that has been
    through a set of qualification
    questions and fits an organisation's
    ideal customer profile) 11, 14, 16,
    17, 22, 26, 30, 49, 65, 66, 99, 101,
    110, 127, 140, 144, 146, 147–8,
    153, 166, 177, 208
psychographic and behavioural
    considerations, customer 103–4
public information, market
    knowledge and 87–8

questions to ask and why 129,
    136–9, 147

referrals 144, 149, 168–9, 197
rejection, dealing with 29–32, 36, 47,
    50, 55, 58, 67–8, 115
relationship established, sales process
    and 144, 149

relationship management (CRM)
    system, customer 7, 25, 86, 130,
    131, 145, 154–5, 164, 210
retail 108, 157, 191–4
retargeting 172
RFxs 189–90

sacking a customer 222, 235–6
sales process 4, 7–8, 11, 16, 17, 18, 21,
    22, 25, 37, 46, 48, 49, 51, 56, 60, 63,
    74, 76, 82, 97, 99, 100, 102, 103,
    107, 109, 110, 111, 127, 129–56,
    157, 159, 161, 163, 170, 176, 183,
    187, 188, 191, 194, 195, 196, 199,
    200, 207, 210, 211, 212, 213–14,
    215, 217, 222, 229, 236, 237
    basis of a good 129, 130–6
    closed questions/open questions
        136–7
    committed prospect 147–8
    conclusion/decision ('Obtaining
        Commitment') 133–4
    customer needs discovered 144,
        147
    customer relationship
        management (CRM) system
        154–5
    existing customers and 229
    how to approach 14–17
    implementation, launch and
        handover 149
    implication questions 138, 139,
        143
    introduction ('Preliminaries')
        132
    is there a fit? ('Demonstrating
        Capability') 133
    likely customer 148–9
    made contact 144, 145–6
    management time focus in 129,
        150
    monitor, upsell and continuation
        149

need–payoff questions 139
objections 141–3
opportunities/fallbacks 145
problem questions 137–8
proposal, role of 151–4
prospective customer won't go
    through 150–1
questions to ask and why 129,
    136–9
relationship established 149
sample 129, 143–9
situation questions 137
uncovering motive
    ('Investigating') 132–3
sales roles 43–70
    account manager and see account
        management
    business development 52–70
    hiring 44–5
    holding out for the right person
        58–9
    hunter, the/'closer' 47–50, 51, 52,
        56, 65, 66, 67, 68, 72, 75, 230
    interview questions 60–70
    new business/'hunting' 46–52
    pre-sales/'opener' 50–2, 100, 184
    types of salespeople needed for a
        business 45–52
situation questions 137, 142
social media 51, 82, 86, 90, 94, 96,
    101, 154, 155, 161, 164, 168, 179,
    181, 213, 219
    lead generation and 165–6
    for targeting 183–5
software tools 69, 164, 166–7
star customers/partners 222, 237–8
storytelling 35–6
strategic relationships 54, 111–12,
    222, 233–5
subscriptions and tools, lead
    generation and 165, 167, 175
suspect (organisation that on the
    surface could be a potential

customer but has not been
    matched to the seller's ideal
    customer profile) 11, 22, 49,
    65, 66, 99, 101, 144, 145, 166

targeting 7, 46, 67, 96, 99, 100, 157,
    164, 165, 169, 172, 175–91
    cold calling and 185–6
    email and 179–80
    entertainment and 189
    networking and 178–9
    notes and 177
    social media for 183–4
    tenders and RFxs 189–90
    trade shows and conferences
        187–8
    who to target 175–6
tenders 67, 189–90
trade shows 27, 89, 97, 153, 170,
    187–8
trading, deals and 203–7

upselling 149, 230, 231, 232

value see pricing

websites
    company promotion and 93–4
    lead generation and 165–6, 167,
        171
    retargeting and 172

A Personal Message from the Author

Thank you for reading this book. I hope it has been a valuable and, ultimately, business-changing experience for you. It is my pleasure to share my experience and I hope it leads to great success for you.

However, life in any sales activity within the Information Age is changing fast and, of course, I am still learning, too. Hopefully, you have already taken a look at the blog which is referred to throughout this book. Here I hope to capture future input on all the topics of the book and share any further information to help you. If you haven't, please visit www.salestribe.blog and get involved.

I would also welcome any feedback.

Happy selling and best wishes,

Steve Schrier

Acknowledgements

I would like to give my heartfelt thanks to all the people who have supported me in writing this book. It has been in my head for such a long time and I really appreciate their support in bringing it to life. From a seemingly easy task it has become one of the most challenging things I have done. And I couldn't have done it without you:

Wendy, Olivia and Arthur.

Chris Ash, Patricia Bacon, Simon Bernholt, Mark Cranstoun, Ian Hogg, David McDowell, Alan McLaughlin, John Welch, Hans Winkelman, Gale Winskill.

And the team at Unbound.

About the Author

STEVE SCHRIER has been in multinational commercial roles for 25 years in the technology sector, including the UK and the Bay Area of San Francisco. Steve has been on the journey from start-up to exit several times in his career and focuses on high business growth through proven commercial engagement techniques.

Unbound is the world's first crowdfunding publisher, established in 2011.

We believe that wonderful things can happen when you clear a path for people who share a passion. That's why we've built a platform that brings together readers and authors to crowdfund books they believe in – and give fresh ideas that don't fit the traditional mould the chance they deserve.

This book is in your hands because readers made it possible. Everyone who pledged their support is listed below. Join them by visiting unbound.com and supporting a book today.

Catherine Aithal
B Aitken
Igor Andronov
Mikael Ångman
Chris Ash
Amir Askarov
Raja B-Sheikh
Jason Ballinger
Stuart Banks
Simon Bernholt
J Besso
H Bhajan
Erik Bhullar
M Birch
Marc Burroughes

Edward Byard
Daniel Camilleri
Justin Chamberlain
Mark Cranstoun
Gal Dayan
Dizzy Dezille
Paul Dolman-Darrall
Craig Driver
Gal Ehrlich
Will Elmwood
Tom Filby
O Florence
Emma Gale
John Gordon
P Harvey

Ian Hogg
Mads Jensen
Sam Johnson
Dan Kieran
Ann Kl
Timothy Lawrenson
Jordan Levin
Craig Luke
@macbet
A McCole
Julie McCole
David McLeish
Peter Miles
John Mitchinson
Carlo Navato
Jacqui Nolan-Neylan
Keith Oloughlin
Sovanna Phan

Michael Phelan
Dan Phillips
Robert Picard
Justin Pollard
Andrew Porter
Christian Rajter
Gil Rotem
Ashley Sandyford-Sykes
David Sargeant
Russell Schrier
Andy Stubley
A Thomas
Marcela Torres
Catherine Turner
Tõnu Vahtra
Willem van Oort
Lee Williams
Mr Med Yukon